D1927788

My Mind My Master: The Eternal

Hratch Ogali, Mind Instructor

Clink Street

London | New York

Published by Clink Street Publishing 2016

First edition.

ISBN: 978-1-911110-69-9 PAPERBACK
978-1-911110-70-5 EBOOK

Contents

Foreword

In 2004, I visited Hratch Ogali's Mind Clinic in London, England, which treats a variety of neurological and other disorders. The clinic's underlying philosophy of consciousness-driven healing is difficult to understand through conventional, body-focused biomedical concepts, but, nevertheless, resonates with the wisdom inherent in many of the world's older mind-body-spirit healing traditions.

Although I'm a product of the mainstream biomedical establishment, including holding numerous senior-level, policy-making positions, my visit convinced me that Hratch is a gifted healer, who has acquired many invaluable insights that need to be better integrated into our healing armamentarium.

Although Hratch stresses rigorous physical rehabilitation like others, he emphasizes a shift in patient consciousness. For example, in the case of spinal cord injury, he catalyses and reinforces a shift from the defeating 'you-will-never-walk-again' attitude that is deeply imprinted in consciousness after injury to a positive, 'Yeah, I will do it.' When this new attitude is embedded with conviction in our consciousness, the captain of our ship – the physical body – starts to follow. Hratch's role is catalytic; he is not the healer but the force that opens the prison door allowing the patient to step through if so desired. Patients heal themselves, starting from the deepest soul level.

As a dyslexic, Hratch's insights come from a different view of the universe to that of conventionally trained doctors and scientists, who acquire much of their knowledge through scholarly reading. Denied traditional sources of knowledge, Hratch's intuitive insights came from years of extensive contemplative meditation. Although Western science eschews such a process, ancient cultures embraced it as the only effective way for obtaining higher-level insight. Perhaps reflecting the inner peace that accrues from such cumulative meditation, Hratch has a gentle, almost sage-like attitude when interacting with patients. He treats them with love and develops what seems to be a soul intimacy that creates the connection needed to generate healing in consciousness.

Like most of my mainstream scientific colleagues, I once embraced a mechanistic model of healing which essentially views the body as a summation of parts – whether they are molecules, cells, organs, or cord to be fixed in isolation of an overriding, integrating consciousness. Although the scientific community disdains mind-body-spirit healing, in a-rose-by-any-other-name fashion, it is grudgingly acknowledged in a more scientific-sounding discipline called psycho-neuroimmunology, which, to some degree, conceptually represents the same thing – i.e. how attributes of consciousness affect health.

The role of consciousness in healing has always been troublesome for scientists. Unlike neuroscientists who tend to equate consciousness with brain chemistry and biology, many alternative healers view the brain as merely the body's physical processor for consciousness. Under this view, although outward expression of consciousness may be a function of the processor's neuronal synaptic connections, etc., it is not the site of consciousness any more than your big toe is.

With such beliefs, even if our brain is damaged by injury or disease, our consciousness is always whole and complete, and possesses the blueprint memories of our able-bodied selves that can be accessed for healing. However, all the negative attitudes and emotions that may have been picked up interfere with accessing these healing blueprints. Like burrs sticking to Velcro, these beliefs are difficult to eliminate and, unfortunately, often imposed by our medical professionals. For example, when a cancer patient is told that he has only six months to live, he, indeed, often dies after that time period because that expectation has been imprinted in his consciousness by an authority figure.

In another example, the imprint is even deeper for spinal cord injury because it is based on medicine's cumulative historical experience for the disorder and not the ever-growing possibilities of the future. Patients are told that they will never walk again and any thoughts otherwise will just prevent them from getting on with their lives. This is a tough, deeply imprinted sentence that must be surmounted to have any significant physical healing. It is like trying to push a car in one direction (i.e. healing the physical body) when the steering wheel (i.e. your consciousness) is cranked in another direction. Any healing modality will work better when the steering wheel is turned in the right direction – basically, Hratch's goal.

A key element to Hratch's program is a guided meditation session, the purpose of which is to establish a one-to-one communion of consciousness between Hratch and patient. In my case, although I have meditated for years, I have rarely gone into a deeper, trance-like state. It is in such a receptive state that Hratch begins the process of busting apart negative belief patterns that inhibit physical healing.

In conclusion, Hratch's program reflects healing wisdom espoused by mankind through most of history until the emergence of modern medicine and its aversion to consciousness-related healing influences. Given that most of us intuitively understand that our consciousness, will and resulting attitudes affect the outcome of whatever we strive for, ranging from athletic performance to rehabilitation, Hratch's healing insights make a lot of common sense.

Dr Laurance Johnston is funded by the Paralyzed Veterans of America (PVA) to research and write about therapies that expand the healing spectrum for individuals with physical disabilities, especially spinal cord dysfunction. He is the former director of PVA's Spinal Cord Research and Education Foundations. Previous to this, he was a Division Director at the US National Institutes of Health and a regulatory official at the US Food and Drug Administration.

1 Why this book?

Success begins in the mind

"When you put your mind to it you can accomplish anything."

This is a phrase often used yet seldom understood. What is the mind? How is it possible to accomplish 'anything'?

Look around you, and you will find individuals who have achieved great things in their lives. They may claim that they were merely lucky, yet you know they have worked hard to achieve their goals.

Your goal, or purpose, must be your starting point; and your true goal must be concordant with the wishes of your unconscious mind. Many go aimlessly through life not knowing what their purpose is. Since they have no worthwhile goal to aim for, they are unlikely to achieve much. A lucky few come across their goal quite late in life. Only then do they recognise that this is what they were searching for all along.

You may be among those who finds your way by trial and error, but the main elements of your success are no different from anyone else's. You too have to work hard towards your goal, to focus, to be committed and determined, to use the power of will, to endure misfortune along the way and most importantly, to be patient.

Self-examination

This book is the result of fourteen years of self-questioning.

I was looking for answers to the mysteries in my own life. How can I overcome my difficulties? Why do I feel this way? Where is it leading me? Where is the fairness in life? What is it that I can do? Who is going to save me?

In the course of my self-exploration, I discovered the astonishing abilities of my own unconscious mind. I was constantly drawn to searching within. Whenever I searched for knowledge I journeyed into the darkness of the unconscious and these visits took me to the beginning of life and time where I rediscovered my innate understanding. All my personal questions led me to the universal questions of life.

All of us at some point during our existence ask for answers to the most fundamental questions. My studies inspired me.

The answers lie within

This need and desire to understand myself was a part of my nature; and I concluded that this same yearning is within all of us, and is available to all of us, if we choose to find it.

Time and again it became clear to me that the human mind possesses all the answers. With focus and commitment I developed psychic ability, telepathic ability and healing ability. I retrieved information and abilities from my unconscious mind by literally instructing my mind to give me the answers.

My analysis widened. I began to consider how it could be applied to our present state as a species, to what we have become and how we function within our environment. My mind gave me answers that were relevant to all living things. I now had a desperate urge to inform everyone of my findings.

Correct actions receive the mind's consent

Over the years, people who seek change have crossed my path. Many feel torn between religion, tradition and their own inner nature. In all cases I find that those who choose to respect their instinctive sense of what is right for them, rather than be ruled by tradition or religion or other social pressures, will benefit and begin to see their way forward.

Every individual I work with experiences life changes brought about, in the first instance, by changes in perception. Those who are unwell learn to put their minds to their emotional and physical disabilities, however severe. They learn to see reason: that is, to search deep inside themselves to find out what they unconsciously knew all along – that their mental or physical, or sometimes even their spiritual, pain is a manifestation of something in their lives that is not quite working in harmony with the rest.

I have discovered that by seeking within, and instructing the mind with determination and commitment, almost any physical or psychological weakness can be overcome.

The method

It is difficult to define what I actually do. In my consulting room is equipment for use by the physically disabled, but none of it is of any use without a committed mind. What takes place within the mind of the person I am counselling will always seem mysterious. I only know how I interpret it to myself: my goal is to instruct the person's unconscious mind to work with their physical brain to create change.

So how is it that I can instruct someone else's mind? You know, as I do, how hard it seems to instruct one's own, never mind someone else's. If we all did what's good for us, the world would be a better place. Yet every day, people choose to ignore 'what's good for them'. Have you ever made a choice 'against your own better judgement,' and come to regret it? Most people have. Often we don't trust our instincts and yet we know that they are usually valid because our most basic instinct is for self-preservation.

We are all instinctive Mind Instructors. When things go right for you, you look up and murmur 'thank goodness'; in moments of need, you look up and plead 'what on earth shall I do?' You look up because you are thanking your own mind for the decisions it's made or asking your own mind to retrieve the correct solution.

The individuals who come to see me may arrive full of doubt or trepidation or even disbelief. They develop trust and confidence as I lead them in an analysis of their own behaviour patterns. They come to an understanding of what is happening to them, and this in itself is a big change. They can now trust their minds to be receptive; they have accepted that feeling better is a goal they can attain.

Lives lived with real understanding are lives in which people can recuperate emotionally, mentally and physically. My patients seek answers to fundamental questions; they begin to comprehend the mechanism of how they function, and this in turn alters their perception of themselves. Whatever we achieve together is always based on instructions given to the mind.

You, like me, like everyone else, accept an endless stream of instructions from the unconscious. These, if correctly understood and applied, allow you to move forward. Once you have learned how to seek within, to interrogate your own mind, you will be able to instruct it. You will be able to give precise instructions aimed at creating change. You will find that your mind is capable of presenting your body or your consciousness with the correct natural solution. When you have learned to know and trust your own mind, your goals will appear achievable, and you will be free to begin your journey with the end in mind.

Mind instructions have the power to create or influence

transformations that would otherwise be thought impossible. The answers are always in the mind; possess the key that unlocks its wonderful treasures, and you will possess an awareness of your destiny and the control that enables you to reach your goals.

The results

I have never claimed any medical expertise, and since I began to put my theories into practice I have been confronted by people with scores of ailments I have never heard of. Yet whatever the condition I am treating, what I am able to establish is the underlying mechanism of how symptoms establish themselves, and what is required to reverse the process and restore normal healthy functioning. I have applied mind instructions to many people with severe physical, mental and emotional disabilities which the medical profession could not diagnose or treat, and in most cases their own minds have effected an improvement or a cure.

Medical science is still mystified by how this happens. Often the physical effects of disease or accident have been so drastic that a cure is, according to conventional medicine, impossible. After all, if the signals to and from the brain and nerve endings and muscles are not merely dormant but undetectable, how is it that they can regenerate? How can the muscles receive instructions from the brain if there is no detectable physical connection? Yet it happens.

A woman who had been confined to a wheelchair by paralysis was able to get up and take her first steps after less than three months of instruction. A child of thirteen came to me, having been told there was no medical treatment for the way his arm continually became dislocated from its socket. After just eight hours of mind instruction, the arm was back in place, while the child – back at school – accelerated to the top of his class. A woman whose spinal cord had been severed, who had been paralysed for eleven years from the shoulders down, regained movement after six months and was eventually able to take steps. In every case of paralysis that I have treated, regardless of whether the cause has been injury or disease, patients have achieved startling progress.

Cases which doctors have pronounced irreversible have regained some of their former functions. Motor neurone disease sufferers have managed to regain control over their body and understand the mechanism of the disease, enabling them to control their natural functions and maintain balance. People with brain injury who had been comatose began to respond, to move, to breathe more deeply, to make sounds and generally return to life. Others with Parkinson's disease walked normally again after fifteen minutes of mind instruction. Schizophrenics, at least one of whom had been severely ill and hospitalised, have learned to trust their own minds, and live normal lives without a chemical crutch.

My website, mindinstructor.com, will link you to press coverage of individuals whose work with me has liberated them, physically and mentally.

Do I have 'failures'? Of course. But these are rarely the severest cases. They usually occur when there is some hidden benefit to be gained from remaining in physical or mental pain. It is cruel and unreasonable to suggest that someone with a life-threatening or agonising condition does not get better because they 'don't want to.' However, there are other cases where the condition fulfils a psychological need or an emotional dependence. Then, there is a resistance to letting go. Letting go of apparent troubles may reveal far deeper, and even more difficult, problems. Where such an emotional resistance to change exists, people always know, at the level of the mind, that they have within them the capacity to cut their troubles down to size and address the deeper problems. They have simply chosen not to use that capacity.

All those who have the will and determination to work have been able to bring about transformation. They are not always 'cured'; their diseases and injuries are real enough. But their brains, correctly instructed, have adapted to instruct their bodies to accommodate their disease or injury more usefully and to improve their quality of life.

How we adapt

Our capacity to adapt is indisputable. In the very long term, it is called evolution. Within a single human lifespan, we adapt from babyhood to function within our place and time and culture and abilities.

Under normal conditions of good health, our bodies constantly restore and regenerate themselves. Our brains instruct our skin to form scar tissue and our immune system to fight disease. We do not need to will these things to happen; the brain and body work together naturally for the benefit of the whole organism; we 'get better'. But sometimes the injury or disease is so traumatic that the emotions are engaged. We are terrified; we are dismayed; at a deep level we are in shock. This is often true even when a person is born with a disability, for anxiety transmits itself. And in every case the individual must apply the mind to assisting the brain to help the body.

By simply accepting and following instructions to help you along your path in life, you can come to understand and pay attention to your own mind, and exercise your own abilities.

The journey

Everyone who comes to see me has the ability to overcome their own difficulties, provided a desperate drive to succeed is there. I am no longer astonished by the power of the mind to stimulate the brain; but I never underestimate the effort that must be made in getting to know one's own mind. It requires concentration, and determination, and openness to change.

Deep emotions usually surface and must be resolved, otherwise symptoms can recur. Our emotional perceptions are an extremely important aspect of our well-being and must remain healthy and well-directed at all times.

There is no quick fix solution to learning, and full recovery, in every aspect, takes time. This book is not a self-help book; it cannot do the work for you. But with practice and determination, the rewards of embarking upon a journey to true wellness are evident, and the difficulties seem barely noticeable. After months or years, your new skills have become part of you, and you experience real joy from using and improving on your own expertise.

Always remember that the journey is yours, and it is you who travel alongside your guide; it is not the book, not the teacher, but you.

You take that journey for life. The key to mind instruction is clarity of vision: the ability to understand your own inner mind, so that you can instruct it. Learning how to do this is an intensely personal exercise. Its outcome is personal to you.

Awareness must be your starting point. Become aware of what it is within you that is driven by superficial emotions, and what is true; then you can alter your perceptions and your actions accordingly.

Read this book with care, and you will identify your own personal emotional barriers. You will learn ways to overcome whatever is restricting your progress in life. Your experiences will become resources: you will be able consciously to apply what you are learning and to grow and develop to your maximum potential.

Whether you are infirm or perfectly healthy, unless you understand and consult your own basic nature as it manifests itself in your mind, you can never live your life to its fullest potential. By applying the natural methods of mind instruction you will gain a true sense of purpose, and the confidence that the purpose is the right one.

First, accept: your mind is your master.

2 My Mind My Master

The acceptance

I stand here as my mind's servant and my mind. My master is my servant, for the one has to serve the other. As a servant I request that my mind remain active at all times, and that its natural power shall guide me through its memory of information.

My mind is aware and capable of transforming actions at will. My mind responds to my natural will-power. Its fragile complexity and its delicate nature work on my emotions and my physical self. Like them, my mind is potentially extremely powerful, yet helpless without attention.

Within my mind resides the memory of its birth and because my mind is the product of nature, it is dependent on nature, as mother and father. Therefore everything my mind understands and perceives must be absolutely natural and pure for its power to evolve through its cycles of life and death.

My mind requests and demands from life simplicity and purity. When I supply a simple acknowledgement this will activate my mind's power, and the healthier and stronger I shall be. The more attention and acknowledgement I pay to my mind, the more power it will generate and the greater its abilities will be. The knowledge concealed in my mind is far beyond my imagination, although it is easy to fantasise about its implications.

My Mind My Master will demonstrate the natural mechanism of life.

Establishing calm and focus

Calm your mind.

Sit or lie in a position you find relaxing. Breathe in deeply and slowly through your nose and breathe out deeply and slowly through your mouth.

Breathe regularly, deeply, slowly.

Detach your thoughts from the world around you. Concentrate your attention on yourself. Ignore your emotions, ignore your wants, ignore the demands of others. Refuse to accept any intrusions.

Focus your breathing towards clearing your mind.

Close your eyes, and direct your focus into your forehead.

Breathe in deeply and slowly through your nose, and breathe out deeply and slowly through your mouth.

Practise the technique, and you will begin to reach your unconscious mind.

With every breath you take, spring-clean your mind. Throw everything out.

Focus on your objective.

Focus on your thought. Breathe in to the thought.

You are paying attention to it, wanting to understand its purpose. The more you breathe the more focused you become.

Your mind begins to respond to all the issues.

You are calm. Your thoughts are focussed. Concentrate.

You begin to reach a deeper understanding of yourself. Your unconscious mind can alter your behaviour. Changes in behaviour will prepare you for the changes which are necessary to strengthen you, and set you on the road to your goals.

Once in a while take a deep breath.

If your mind asks you to stop, do so.

If your mind is captivated by a particular concept, do not

hurry on and ignore it. Make every effort to be inquisitive. Try to understand why your mind is attracted to this idea. Simply follow the guidance of your mind, free from choices based on emotions.

Emotions and the unconscious mind

As you are a human being, all of your conscious thoughts are mediated by emotion. Emotions inevitably underlie much of your behaviour and many of your reactions. Sometimes you are aware that you are being prompted by negatively sensitive memories or traumas. Perhaps as a result, you will flee from some issue that needs to be addressed, or seek solace where your own better judgement tells you that none is to be found. If so the emotional trauma remains unresolved.

None of your motivating wishes and desires, whether they lie deep down or are close to the surface of your consciousness, whether they are fruitful or damaging, are native to your unconscious mind. Rather have they been overlaid upon the pure essence of your unconscious, which was there before you began to develop in the world. Your unconscious mind understands your emotions, yet can accommodate them in harmony only when your consciousness is free of barriers and fears.

Faced with what is unworthy and unproductive, the unconscious mind reacts. If its reaction is deeply negative, it can affect those functions of your brain which normally operate at a level beyond your consciousness: the combined functions of organs and muscles and brain response that should operate to keep your body in good working order.

Balance

As a human being you have a spirit and mind (your unconscious) and a brain and emotions (your consciousness). Your conscious and unconscious cannot work without each other. They possess equal amounts of energy. With this energy they can work positively or negatively; they can act in your interests as an organism, or contrary to those interests.

Creating a balance between positive and negative depends upon the way you make your choices in life, and the degree to which you understand your own emotions. Like the left and right side of your physical body, your conscious and unconscious constituents must work together so that you can achieve balance and move forward.

When you learn to focus on your unconscious mind, the results begin to show as you bring your conscious into balance with it. You achieve self-awareness and control. Once balance is achieved, you can begin to instruct your mind to change the way you think. Your weaknesses will be dismissed and your strengths fully utilised.

Interaction with the world

You experience life selectively. You select what to see and hear and smell according to what your mind projects into your environment as well as according to what you receive from it. Your selection is conveyed to your unconscious mind, but so is a great deal that you did not consciously select.

Eventually, all the impressions will surface as thoughts. Then you recognise that you have options and can choose between them. You want to identify the option that will best assist you to achieve your goal. However, if your impressions are confused by emotion, you will find it hard to know which way to turn: there will be muddle and stagnation. Now you must interrogate your unconscious mind. Clarify which choices will really assist you along your path, and you will attain the ultimate truth, the correct way to proceed.

If you accumulate unresolved thoughts, that is, thoughts muddled by emotion which linger between the conscious and the unconscious mind without conclusion or direction, these will become troublesome. If you then fuel them with still more upsetting emotion, the resulting chaos and confusion may result in physical or mental breakdown.

The short thread

There is a short thread between the unconscious mind and correct action.

You were born with the instinct to survive. But as a social animal, you have empathy. Your mind does not tell you to act without consideration for others. You must act according to your natural level of volition – the short thread – wherever you can. This means being in touch with your mind and clearing it of emotional obstacles. Only then will you achieve balance between being yourself and being a creature of emotion.

You may feel that no survival technique can help you, for your body is unwell or immobile. But if your senses are present and any part of your brain is there, there is nothing that the mind cannot do. It has so much power. Science is still examining the strange facility of the human brain to use alternative parts of itself, when one part has been forcibly shut down. Damaged lines of communication between brain and body can sometimes be restored, and it is the mind which has to instruct your brain to re-connect.

Why would you neglect your mind?

Perhaps you strive to modify and improve your own appearance. And you want to live a long life: you eat healthily, avoid polluting your body, exercise to keep your muscles toned, take classes to improve your mental agility.

But what you really need is true personal fulfilment, which can only emerge from the capacity to instruct your mind.

This too takes effort. You will need a balanced, accurate view of your fears and weaknesses, as well as your strengths and resilience. With honest self-assessment, which is the only way to become truly self-reliant, you will be genuinely optimistic. Your optimism will be based on your ability to make fruitful decisions, free of emotional obstacles.

You will keep your goal clearly in sight, and will know what you have to do to get there, and how you will use your huge capacity to learn.

Your external reality will have sense and direction. You will cease to be overwhelmed by the immediate and the visible; you will learn from every moment of your experience. You will make mistakes only once, learn from each mistake, and move forward.

Your unconscious mind will provide you with answers, and in so doing will help you become healthier and wiser.

Empowerment, protection, motivation

The spirit within your mind, the spirit within you, is unique. Its purpose is to empower you, to protect you, and to motivate you to act as part of humankind which is constantly evolving through action. The power of your spirit is pure; it is part of nature, as you are; the passion of your spirit is the ultimate passion and its source is the energy that sustains the universe, continually repeating the cycles of physical and spiritual life and balancing all through magnetic force.

Spiritual purity can be represented by the extremes of positive and negative magnetic energy. Those who fulfil their path in life in an uncorrupted, mindful manner, move their position towards the lighter, the positive.

Energy generates light. The further we move away from the energy of our spirit, the darker it will become.

Where light and dark meet, at that point our minds affect our physical being; and in turn, the physical being builds and preserves your healthy mind. By exercising your abilities and using your creativity to the limits you improve; you learn; you find it easier to reach the real spirit within you. From now on, your actions enlighten the human species.

3 True Spirituality

Religion: a human construct

The spiritual world cannot be quantified for it spans the entire universe. Your innate spirituality is true and pure, so you have nothing to fear. The confusion between spirituality and religion may trouble you, because religion is based on emotional choices and spirituality on the pure mind, which possesses the ultimate power. Spiritual freedom is natural, while religion is constructed. It is organic, while religion is man-made.

Indigenous tribes in less industrialised parts of this earth thrive under the influence of the spirits. They are advised by a wise man or shaman who consults the spirits and obeys their instructions. You too can reach higher levels of understanding by entering and re-entering the spiritual world in search of wisdom. Only when you have reached deep into the mind and its memory will you be fully aware that these spiritual dimensions exist, and possess ultimate wisdom that can be applied to the situation in which you find yourself.

All religions claim that there is life after death. You may have faith that life after death exists and in your desperate moments you turn to the spiritual for attention and help. Your unconscious journeys into the inner spiritual world can be made only with your mind's permission and with obedience.

Only your mind itself can allow you to reach a deeper understanding of its own existence and purpose.

True Spirituality

You probably talk about your god; you may have an inner awareness about the existence of a divine or greater power that is hidden from the physical, and is deemed to be just, possessing the answers to all your prayers, hopes and discontentment. Throughout time human beings have striven to make contact with a higher power. Whether you are a believer or not, at moments of need you will turn, whether outwardly or inwardly, towards one saviour or many.

When we are at our most vulnerable we begin to search for answers, to search for the meaning of life, whether this is through organised religion, or through self development. At such times you are introduced to the idea of a god, a divine power that can make or break you. God is just a word – a human construct to describe whatever you think it is: whether a human form, a superior energy, or simply an inner awareness of another existence.

The only place you need to search for 'god' is in your mind. There you can reach beyond your physical self and enter the darkness, to search for the light which contains the answers and the knowledge you want.

When you do this, you may come to believe that what you achieve comes from beyond and is almighty. However you interpret the wisdom you receive, it is available to you, at moments of need, so long as you have learned to perceive your own inner power and truth. This is the ultimate truth, in your physical life or your spiritual; it lies within your natural unconscious memory as a distant recollection that can only be reached through conscious effort and desire. It is unconnected to any particular religious belief, so you must clarify within your own mind the dividing line between religiousness and godliness.

Liberation

For a moment take a step ahead of religion. Let religion fall into your memory without suffering the guilt of detachment, and begin to experience the natural transition of your thought towards freedom.

Religion is from the past and has served its purpose. Understand whatever prejudices, restrictions and limitations your religion has inflicted upon you. People have participated in religions throughout history. Religion has presented rules and boundaries which were laid down many centuries ago in teachings devised at a time and place far removed from your own. Maybe you have accepted these rules as part of your life, but it is now time for you to enter into direct communication with godliness. Observe the changes within; you will feel free. You have not rejected spirituality; you have simply chosen to ignore the creators of religion.

The door to your own godliness will open to you as enter your mind without carrying the burden of religion. You will be drawn towards situations and people that will lead you to self-fulfilment. Your personal path may lead you to give humanity something new, simply to lead a fuller life, or to help others directly. Whatever the choices you make, you will be sure that they are those of your own mind, and that the purpose being followed is your own purpose, and you are not merely acting out the wishes and aims of others.

Drive

Whether or not you believe in reincarnation, you know that your true spirit is beyond the physical. In this physical life you lead, your spirit demands that you make progress. It demands that you strive to achieve objectives. You are driven by some inner energy to change and develop as you move forward through time. This energy is your spiritual force, a combination of memory, imagination and your particular nature. Some may call it god, others may call it the human spirit or the soul. Your beliefs will dictate what you call it. All you know is that it is hard to pinpoint, examine and analyse. To do so you must ask your mind for answers, for it is your mind that tells you you have this inner spirit, which can offer strength, wellbeing and balance.

When you ask your mind for an answer, you are searching for a point of view that seems to emanate from somewhere beyond time and space; the spirit that inhabits a situation and allows you to attain a state of mind in which the correct way is clear. In this state of mind you possess a kind of 'sixth sense.' It is important that your spirit should work at the forefront of your mind, for it will remind you always to be thoughtful and to maintain control of your emotions.

4 Embracing life

Being in the world

You are unique. For this reason you must pay attention to yourself in order to understand your own natural abilities. Your strengths and weaknesses make you who and what you are.

Begin by connecting with wider nature; understand the natural world you live in. You do not have to distance yourself from your normal environment. You do not have to become a monk or escape to a mountain or a desert to commune with nature. Your mind is natural; it understands nature. It works with nature. It will not serve you better, or bring you greater peace or any new knowledge, if you are isolated in an empty space or if you search the universe for answers. Nor will it be helped if you appeal to the gods. The longer you wait for a response, the more desperate you will become, and that may cast you into darkness; but that darkness is your mind urging you to think.

Your mind possesses the wisdom of nature, therefore you may benefit from its power at any time or place or stage in life.

The busiest and most effective people are those best connected with their own inner reality. Your internal lines of communication with your mind should be open at all times. First begin to explore and understand your memory. You will discern how your consciousness is founded in emotions, and you will perceive what your mind at a level below consciousness is telling you.

Avoiding engagement with the mind

Your mind is always active, constantly analysing your situation to provide you with the most logical and appropriate solution. You may hear its wisdom from 'the back of your mind' at times of difficulty, but dismiss, ignore or deliberately avoid it. This is because the physical fulfilment of your senses makes you adventurous, yet extremely vulnerable. You choose to pursue false, emotionally driven pride and begin to drive yourself into a trap. Often, fortunately, your mind becomes more active and you cannot avoid the mind's truth; it tells you how to rescue yourself and you take correct action and you are saved. At other times your mind may find that your emotional struggle is a too great a threat to its continued existence. It then deserts you; it appears to die, but before its death, it leaves behind a memory that will be brought to life once more. Because all living things mimic their own species, we mimic in response to the imprint that a mind leaves behind; and thus the human unconscious evolves.

You have an active mind and you live at a time where your environment is rapidly changing. This presents new challenges which you naturally enjoy meeting. But sometimes your actions will take you to dark places, and you become confused as you try to find reason between the way things should be and the way they are.

Remember the way that things *should be* does not belong to us in any case. Your environment offers promises, but all too often delivers disillusion. Your decisions and actions must be based, ultimately, on the way things are.

Distractions

How can you understand your own mind and fully exploit its natural energies? First you have to understand your emotional traumas, which you must question and investigate. Here your thoughts must take over. There is a logical explanation for all the emotional decisions you make in the course of the day; be clear what that explanation is.

Whenever you make assumptions based on emotion, you are almost certainly wrong. Just think about assumptions of that kind that you've made in the past. Maybe you were hoping to please another person, or to conform in a way that was contrary to your inner nature. Weren't these emotions just creative fantasies, based on the desires and anxieties you had at the time? And isn't it true that they were mostly mistaken? Now think about those that did turn out to work for you, and you will find that you were really acting out of an instinctive awareness of a positive outcome.

Once you analyse the emotions that have determined your mistakes of the past, your mind can take over in future, and remind you to base your judgement on reality and your own personal truth.

To achieve a higher level of understanding, write your thoughts down on paper and begin to identify what is emotional and what is not. You will find that when you ask your mind a question, it will begin to answer. This practice of connecting to the power of your mind will become routine, and when it does the quality of your life will improve. You will gain serenity and endurance, born of a greater understanding of what you are truly capable of.

Your abilities

As a human being you can be patient. You have the gift of endurance; it is in your nature as an organism to stay alive and to flourish, to move on from negative events and people and remain active in mind, body and spirit.

You can learn to know yourself. This means you will travel through life with wisdom, the greatest help of all on any journey.

You can decide to think well of others wherever possible.

You can adjust to circumstances and to the people and materials at hand.

You can use the power of your mind to reach objectives.

You can understand the value of giving and receiving.

You can give unconditional help to those who are in need.

So long as you have breath in your body, *you can*. So long as your breath sustains your life then you can move forward, spiritually, mentally or physically. Learning how best to follow life's path exercises your natural abilities and your willpower.

You can learn to visit your mind with ease, to become one with your mind so that your natural abilities and will are never suppressed. Practise: always pay attention to your mind. You will trust yourself more, and feel safer when you make decisions; you will fully embrace the potential of your life.

Learning

Have you ever said 'I can't'? This negativity is an unnatural, learned reaction. As an organism you have been moving forward and developing since the sperm impregnated the egg. Why should you question your own ability?

The missing factor is attention. If you find it hard to focus on an area of interest, then of course you feel unable to deal with it. However this is only a judgement, not a fact, and a negative judgement at that. You can more usefully judge it necessary to develop curiosity about the subject and the mental energy to understand it fully.

When reason tells you that you are curious and can understand, then you develop your ability to the full. Arm yourself with a battery of achievements, and life becomes easier.

Abilities and and willpower work together at the deepest level. Your unconscious and conscious challenge you all the time, and you need to be able to use both effectively by asking your mind for answers. When your will is liberated from emotional ties and allied to mental ability it thrives.

Those who under-estimate their own abilities abuse their own potential. In the worst cases this may make them strike out in frustration against other people or the world in general. All the energy that goes into these negative abusive thoughts and actions would be better directed towards cultivating understanding and passing on wisdom to others.

Giving and taking

Give generously, for the pleasure it gives and the peace it will bring you. Never promise to give more than you can, for this will only disappoint others and leave you feeling inadequate. Do not give unless you are asked to, as what you give will mean nothing to others and their carelessness will wound you. Do not give to impress, as to do so leaves others feeling inadequate, and is a manifestation of false pride.

Never take what does not belong to you. It hurts others, as it would hurt you; and it diminishes you.

Humans, the destructive species

To have a strong sense of self-worth, you need to consider how you behave in life and in society; and immediately you find yourself troubled by the march of human history. As a species, we notoriously tamper with the earth's ecosystem. Human beings are the most intelligent and advanced life on this planet, yet it is the way we behave that is more likely than anything else to disrupt nature. We suppress the earth's natural energies by polluting and destroying the environment and its residents. Imagine that the earth were an individual in your care; observe the state it's getting into. How does this make you feel?

As a thoughtful individual, you will be aware of the extent of our abuse of the environment. Many people are now struggling to save the planet from destruction, while others allow themselves to keep on laying waste to the environment. They live in pursuit of material gain, at best ignorant of the damage they do and at worst deliberately negligent.

Our planet reacts with violence. Natural catastrophes occur with increasing frequency, and will continue to do so until the life-giving value of the Earth becomes a concern of everyone.

You wish to embrace life and all the Earth has to offer, and leave it a better place. You can bring about changes in your own behaviour, and become more fully alive by challenging those who work to the detriment of the earth, its inhabitants and our existence. When this planet is gone, life is gone. We are born as one and we will die as one.

Contentment

To be contented you do not need to look to a god, but only within yourself, to your own mind. Your mind is your master and it is capable of providing you with all that you need to serve your purpose. Within each mind there is a journey to follow and a unique contribution to make.

If we were all wealthy, wealth would have no meaning or value. If we were all rulers, there would be no-one to rule, and if we were all road-sweepers there would be nothing to sweep. You are unique, as are your abilities. The opportunities you encounter and the talents you have are to be exploited humbly and effectively so that they may serve a true purpose. Using your talents and opportunities is the most important aspect of your life's journey.

Accept others as you would like to be accepted. Material

superiority serves no purpose, and nor does mental or social superiority. Replace a desire for superiority with motivation to reach objectives. You are unique, but no-one can be entirely independent, and you need others as they need you. Listen, and you will identify with others, and learn from them. Other people's experiences are only superficially different from your own. Wherever and whenever we live in the world, we confront the same emotional dilemmas and have the same desires and fears.

Sacrifice your beliefs and have an open mind. What you are about to receive will always be different from anything you imagine.

Messengers

Sometimes on your journey through life you will encounter people, or even events, that come into your life, affect it in some way, and then depart. You may have been mystified by the random chain of cause and effect that led events to happen or brought people to your door. There is nothing to wonder at; luck has no bearing on the fact that these things happen, and nor does 'coincidence' as coincidence implies rarity. There is nothing rare here; random chance makes messengers appear in everyone's lives. What matters is the way you receive yours.

Among the messengers you encounter, there will be angels or devils in disguise. They may bring unforeseen changes and challenges which seem to overwhelm your force of will. Transformations imposed upon you by chance may be painful emotionally, physically or even socially. Alternatively, you may have such 'good fortune' that your feet don't touch the ground, and you are driven off course. In both cases, understand that everything has an end as well as a beginning. All that happens is part of the cycle of your life, and all cycles are important constituents of your self. Everything you learn can be taken forward into the future.

Where transformations are unwelcome, there may be a need to alter your expectations. Remain focussed on the lessons you are learning rather than measuring the speed of your progress towards a goal.

5 The power of the mind

The depth of your own resources

Your unconscious mind can show you the way to overcome all life's obstacles and complications. The deeper you reach, the more empowered you will become, mentally, emotionally, physically and spiritually.

Learning to get in touch with the unconscious mind helps you to identify the correct daily actions to make, and reactions to have. You are a genius within, and like all those who are willing to develop contact with their own mind, you are capable of developing psychic and telepathic and healing powers; insights and capacities that most people attribute only to mystics or to the gifted can become yours.

Your mind's complexity is also its simplicity. Your mind is natural, it is born with you, and it strongly rejects whatever is imposed against your will. It simply cannot sustain or absorb anything that clashes with its logic and its memory. It reacts to your commands, when it is instructed with precision. Given well-directed instruction and deep attention, it can activate senses from the depth of its memory bank. The unconscious mind possesses knowledge far beyond your perception of your true abilities.

Your mind rejects what will not work

Be alert to the mind's resources when you meet people. When you encounter another person it is the hidden communication that takes place first. It is as if two people scan the bar-code of one another to decide whether the communication will be positive or negative; you silently gauge and measure. You may feel uncomfortable with the person you are with, or experience a sensation that may translate into threat. On the other hand, you may be with a person who makes you feel comfortable, almost humbled.

This kind of communication is routine and most people go through it every day. But your mind possesses an active hidden energy that remains constant. These energies extend much, much further and are capable of travelling within the field of magnetic energy that connects all living things, extending to the atmosphere and the universe beyond. Your mind analyses and calculates constantly, every nanosecond, in order to preserve your being. It is simply working to carry out embedded instruction. You have to open communication with your mind and give instruction to allow it to help you become healthier and stronger in mind and body. Above all, you must learn to understand those emotions which can lead you into a chaotic state, where you can degenerate and deplete your body of energy; these emotions are those the mind rejects.

Self-discipline and will-power

Self-discipline and will-power work together; the will is an emotional function and discipline comes from your mind.

Discipline necessarily requires system: doing things in a particular order, often at a particular time. You can discipline yourself to go to sleep and wake up at certain times, for instance; you can discipline your mind to be accessible when you are awake and when you are asleep. You can discipline yourself to run for half an hour every morning, and to to clear your desk every night. Once you have accommodated a particular discipline it becomes habitual and for so long as it is useful to you, it is worth maintaining.

Target-setting is a good discipline, since it teaches you to pay attention to detail and to be alive to opportunities. If you have a clear idea of the goal you're aiming for, you'll be alert to ways of achieving it; if you haven't, opportunities are fumbled and lost and never given your full attention.

In this way, self-discipline helps you to *pay attention.* Your mind is open to stimuli and you make a conscious effort to store and use and retrieve all the useful observations you come across in the course of the day.

If you don't apply self-discipline as a matter of course, you are prone to repeated failures of the will; and if you become conscious of yourself as a 'weak-willed' person, you feel susceptible and vulnerable and start to punish yourself. This is a downward spiral. Your thoughts stagnate and you either take no interest in the people and environment you live with, or you constantly carp and complain and sneer about them and feel sorry for yourself.

None of this works. You need to develop self-discipline, in order to create the order within which your will can work.

Using focussed breathing, interrogate your mind about your motivation and the strength of your desire to accomplish whatever your will can be applied to.

Still breathing deeply, focus on the objective you have in mind.

Your energy is now directed at this and the emotional blockages are removed from your will.

Communicate the changes you need to make in your habits and attitudes.

Your will, at its strongest, allows your mind to create the necessary changes right away.

You are now on the correct path.

Incorporate your aims into your normal mental disciplines.

Making changes

For every moment of unhappiness saved, a life is saved. If you are feeling victimised or unhappy or discontented, ask your mind exactly why that is, and what you will have to change to make yourself happier.

For most people, accepting the possibility of change is the hard part. If you are like this, one part of you will say 'you should change' and the other will say 'yes but...'

It is so much easier *not* to change. There are always reasons why you 'can't'. You're stuck for somebody else's sake; or you fear disaster; or you doubt your own ability.

These are excuses. They are beguiling, sometimes so beguiling that your emotions create a pain. This succeeds in making change harder than ever. Your emotions can even create a pain that is designed to make it impossible for someone else to move on; perhaps you are not being consciously manipulative, but your pain is designed to prevent the change in your own life that will result when another person makes changes in theirs.

Listen to your mind. If your mind tells you to make a difficult change, make it; if in your mind you know that someone else must make a change, let them. Work out the worst thing that can happen, and the best. Plan to limit the damage and to maximise the benefit, but go ahead and take the necessary steps.

One of the hardest things to admit is that *you have been here before.* If you are resistant to change, you will keep finding yourself in the same dead-end situations because you are afraid to break your emotional circle. You are imprisoned by fears which are groundless. Maybe this is a fear of hurt, or loss of face, or loss of money. Appropriate fear is a perfectly natural self-protective mechanism and it is necessary; but the consequences of not dealing with exaggerated fears are much, much worse. Take things logically. Write down what would happen *if.* Write down what you would do *if.* Now write down what will happen if the fearful monsters don't materialise. Think how you can make your change and avoid them. Think how you will confront them if you have to. The more you think about your monsters, the more easy it becomes to reduce them to their proper size.

If you open your mind to a higher understanding of your own emotions and motives you can make these changes. Your difficulties will disintegrate; you will feel calmer because you know your own fears and can deal with them. If you find yourself repeating mistakes, stop.

Justice

When you are born, you acquire equity: the right to life. You have as much right to be here and enjoy the fruits of the earth as anyone else; and yet you must balance your rights and desires against those of other people. Unless you live in an extremely uncomplicated society your whole life reflects this, in one way or another. It is a struggle for justice, for balance between your rights and desires and those of others.

Justice is supposed to be impartial, disinterested, dispassionate. But you are protective of your own share, and make your own judgement about what is fitting for you; you are supposed to be impartial, disinterested, and dispassionate but your own emotions are involved. How can you ever be sure that your judgement about your own rights and desires is fair?

You will need to interrogate your mind. Your emotions must be set aside: especially the emotions of greed and fear. You are not aiming for elation at your own good fortune or resentment in response to injustice. You are aiming for perfect balance and vindication of the truth.

Let your mind decide what is an imaginative construct of your own, and what is true. Let your mind decide what is a prejudice, and what is vanity. Judge yourself bravely and sincerely before you attack others; give yourself credit where it is due, and admit your faults. If you cannot find justice within yourself, you will never find it in others.

If you treat the opportunity to obtain judgement as a competition, with winners and losers, and are determined to win at all costs, your triumph – if you get it – will leave a sour taste. Defeat, on the other hand, will make you resentful and angry.

But if you approach judgement as an opportunity to learn something, you will benefit whatever happens. Defeat must have no place in your mind. Once you learn to trust it completely, your mind will not allow you to feel defeated, but help you to feel you have learned something that you can put to good use in future.

The endless cycle of nature

You are the product of nature. Energy flows through you and you are constantly affected by the changing environment; you are a part of the universe.

As planets and stars explode and disintegrate new ones are born and elements of these planets travel through the universe propelled by their own energy and pulled by gravity. Beginnings and endings are eternal and maintain and sustain the whole of the universe. Our planet has evolved under these natural laws and its own movements naturally cause its structure to alter.

The force that drives the earth remains constant. Volcanic eruptions may devastate the surface yet the inner power of the earth is not diminished. In the same way depth, memory and what we call the mind and the spirit are born and persist forever. You have a core; the core of your being; this is life, the life that is in every living thing. Like the earth you possess inner powers. Although your appearance changes over time your inner energy remains the same.

Your mind gives you the gift of happiness, which excites you, and of self-fulfilment through achievement, which calms you. Your dynamic energies work together in harmony like the negative and positive force fields of a magnet; they pull first in one direction, then back, as the tides are drawn to ebb and flow by the moon. The cycles of the universe are present in the ebb and flow of happiness and creativity in your mind, and like all living things your mind emerges and fades and is reborn.

Events big and small occur in cycles. Your daily routine, the beginning and end of your day, birth and death in your family, your relationships, your working life and your social life go through cycles which may overlap or coincide. With each one you make choices, accepting and effecting closure and creating fresh beginnings.

Relationships begin and end. People cross your path; some will remain in your life for its duration, while others will contribute knowledge or change when it is necessary and then depart, never to be seen again. Sometimes a message from a stranger begins a new cycle, or gives birth to a thought that makes you end a cycle and create a new one.

Everything you do has a beginning and an end, and it is wise to be mindful of this. Every low is followed by a high; lows and highs together drive you forward,

Your moods and perceptions change as you move through the cycles of your existence, and apply new insights gained from experience; but no cycle is ever exactly like the last, and there is always something new to learn.

Purify your mind

If you try to control others by reprimand, demand and command without thinking, you become full of false pride. Should you inflict this treatment on children, you will cause pain and suffering to future generations. Harsh criticism and scorn are fruitless.

You are an intelligent person and can instruct yourself to behave with more consideration. Intelligence is thoughtfulness, and all criticism must be balanced and generous and tempered with understanding. The criticism we value is constructive, not destructive.

By freeing yourself of false pride and other emotions, you release your own true powers of expression. Perhaps you are afraid that your reactions are slow, and you feel somehow threatened unless you scold or chastise on impulse. Yet if you just think, if you give your mind time to consider problems and mistakes in a relaxed and logical and unemotional way, you will find permanent changes are possible that will make unpleasantness redundant. If instead of hair-trigger reactions you calm down and use your mind and brain, new thought processes will allow you to make progress instead of fighting the world around you.

6 Creativity

Releasing your imagination

Everything you imagine emerges from what you do, how you behave, and what you naturally want. People dreamed of being able to communicate from a distance long before we had the radio or the telephone or television. Let yourself dream. Imagine you are able to transmit thoughts directly from your mind to the mind of another without the intercession of a machine. It is but one step to believing; and out of self-belief and effort come achievement.

Emotions are the obstacle to contemplation. They also get in the way of communication between one human being and another. Suppose you imagine telepathy. To pursue your capabilities with conviction, to develop those areas of your mind, may feel time-consuming or pointless but it takes less effort than you think. Be open to the mind's potential; do not dismiss your own capacity because you have been taught to do so. As you discover your own mind, you will find freedom within it to understand your own intuition, inspiration and imagination and the purpose to which you can put all these things, which will link you to your own evolution as well as the progress of our planet.

You do not have to be a scientist or a painter, a writer or a musician to use your imagination to create something new.

You will find yourself drawn towards the field of endeavour that best suits your interests and your talents.

Your purpose on Earth

Our planet is the past; our preservation is the present and our evolution is the future. Your mind's purpose is to move forward, helping humankind to develop, and you are constantly striving to make unimpeded creative progress; to eliminate thought processes that are based on emotion, to enable you to reach your destiny. To move forward you must always think from the end; always have your purpose in mind. To understand what that purpose is, you must see clearly your own past and present, as well as your future.

You possess little until you justify your life by producing something, and it is your mind that provides the source of inspiration. You breathe, with your senses you feel and touch and hear and smell and see, and your mind tells you that your presence on earth is of value. Next it enables you to exploit your emotions, from which your mind creates a powerful and constructive life.

Your purpose on earth is to achieve something. When you live in balance with your mind, you are placed in situations where you find opportunity. Thus you are driven towards your goal. This is a natural occurrence with every human being. Events and situations present themselves, sometimes out of the blue, and change your way of life – if you are alert to their possibilities. This is called 'being in the right place at the right time'. Many people may be in the right place and time but only a few, those who are fully in touch with their mind and their objectives, recognise the doors that open before them.

However, in all cases we must strive at all times to use our ability and willpower to achieve and improve our life and refuse to submit to weaknesses or unforeseen circumstances that can place us in difficult situations, which can create discomfort or discontentment, where we feel that we have lost our status in life.

Creating change

Our world has known wars, discrimination, prejudice. Should you judge the past? Should you reject all of it because you envisage a better future? The past is not to be judged; its mistakes are clear, and you are fortunate that you do not have to repeat them.

You will strive to change and improve the world you are in, but nothing around you will change unless you divorce yourself from old perceptions and ways of thinking. There is no point in trying to change those who do not understand that their ways are outdated and no longer useful. They must change in their own time, when their own minds are ready.

Changes reveal themselves over a period of time. You will need patience and endurance to allow change to take root in your mind before it acts on your body and the world around you. You will have to keep your mind open to change, to welcome new ideas, to welcome new experiences and to appreciate the wonder of achievement. Your future will create itself. It is ahead, ready to carry you forward on life's journey.

Your creative mind

As you travel through life, you will find yourself drawn towards certain kinds of encounter. You will find yourself compelled to pay special attention to particular people or activities, artefacts or places. Your mind stores all you are learning in your memory until the whole appears before you as a solution of some kind. You will hear people say 'I felt as if my whole life had led up to this point' or 'it all fell into place'.

This happens unexpectedly, because your mind reasons and

selects constantly. It absorbs experience, analyses, and creates something new from it. When you are paying attention to it, you will engage brain and body to construct what your mind dictates.

Every new impression in your life has the potential for an emotion that leads to a thought that lodges in your mind. With time this thought will come to maturity and materialise as inspiration. As in nature, once all the elements are present a birth takes place.

When you feel inspired by some solution or original insight, you are elated. You want to share it; you seek confirmation from others that it is as extraordinary as you think.

But your inspiration is innocent and immature. As you develop it, it grows into a well-rounded theory or plan or piece of work. This development is a process of questioning, testing and reasoning and must take place in your mind alone. It is personal and belongs to you alone until you have developed it. If you release it into the world too soon, you will stifle this development; you might as well drag a seed from the ground before it has grown into a tree. You owe to others the fruit of your inspiration, not the seed.

Creative conflict

Sometimes your creative process takes place subconsciously, and a fully fledged idea emerges; but more usually, your consciousness will make a contribution. You will consider and observe your idea, looking at it from different points of view and in different lights.

You will think from the end, and decide how to overcome the obstacles that stand in your way.

You will decide what is emotional and what is the product of thought. Every thought you have about something that is important to you will have emotional significance, but against those emotions you weigh validity and possibility.

Your mind makes these calculations unbidden. Then things begin to happen: opportunities are there for the taking. At first you feel stuck, unable to take action because you remain uncertain, but you are forced to think nonetheless. You are breaking emotional bonds. And the moment comes when you suddenly know you are free to act, free to express yourself. When this moment comes, it is like a birth; you have indeed brought into being a new concept or artefact or stage in your own progress through life.

Sometimes, in the course of your long labour, your thoughts feel so burdensome that you are lost. Usually this is because emotions are intruding; you lose sleep as your trapped thoughts go round and round in circles in your mind. Night after night, emotional baggage keeps you awake and your questions remain unanswered. Your daily tasks suffer; you feel distracted and isolated.

If you apply reason to the circle of confusion, you will find the point at which your thought is trapped.

Is there any resolution, any way out? Test the options. First address the physical issue: clear your mind and get some sleep. Once you are again alert, re-think, starting from the end and knowing that the first stage is this decision. Concentrate on the issues that matter to your future, not your past. This is where high aims and ideals are important. Allow your expectations to be driven by your mind, and not by emotions that deplete your will.

Serious issues make you lie awake at night, but if you think, rather than revisit emotional dead-ends, your mind will reach a solution. Your creative journey must be innocent of emotion and your solution even more so.

7 Emotions

Applied emotion

Pure logic is your mind's destiny. Your emotions must be applied purposefully, if you are to commence your journey towards your mind. They can be destructive if allowed to lead you, but creative if correctly applied in accordance with the dictates of your mind.

Analysing your emotions is the first thing you must do when you weigh up the encounters you have through life. When you understand the way you really feel, you will eliminate many false moves and transform your future. Then you will be able to use your mind, brain and body to full capacity.

Your emotions make you sensitive and vulnerable, reacting instantaneously to the slightest suggestion; anything can trigger an emotional reaction, even a simple word or letter, number or colour or scent. Because of your emotions, these things may cause a reaction on any level – mentally, physically or psychically. Your emotions can be taken over without your conscious awareness, so it is important to be self-aware and vigilant at all times. Once you understand how your emotions make you behave, you can understand how to change yourself. All you need is logic, analysis, and action.

Think of a way you would like your behaviour to change.

What was the emotion that led to the dysfunctional behaviour?

When, where and how did this emotion manifest itself?

What was its cause, and what its effect?

Redirecting your emotion to analytical thought is the only method for you to understand your life. Use your emotions as a tool; they are not a curse but a gift. Handled with correct understanding and sensitivity, they become, not a burden, but a finely tuned instrument designed to produce results. In the analysis of emotion lies a way to release your true potential. When you start to apply your emotions for greater understanding, your mind begins to thrive.

Emotion can arouse the genius of your mind

At some point in your life you are likely to face trials that will make you confront desperation. Then you will feel intense emotion, and it is with passion and emotion that you will ask for a solution: how shall I go on? At the eleventh hour, events somehow shape themselves so that you are able to draw from deep within some of the potential of which your mind is capable. You may already have had such an experience. Perhaps you drew on resources you didn't know you had, and you look back and view these events as mysterious, a matter of luck or sheer coincidence.

Perhaps you have not looked for the source of the solution. It could only have been your own mind that shaped events, as it is the only part of you that is aware of your most secret thoughts. You did not realise perhaps that your mind was working on a way to resolve your problem all along. The fruits of its labour sprang into consciousness only when confronted by some danger or threat.

Your mind seems to reach into the depths of your memory and experience to present you with a solution, and this is always the only suitable, correct way forward.

A learned response

Your emotions are influenced by your environment. You learn to feel and express emotions in certain ways, and that manner of expression extends to your inner self. It is impossible to describe the strongest of emotions; it is the way you behave that expresses everything. Highly emotional moments often blind you to gradations of feeling. There is no middle way: you are broken-hearted or ecstatic, furiously angry or overwhelmingly pleased.

You may struggle to find a meaning in your life. Perhaps you see the lives of others and compare them to your own. Maybe you make comparisons in an attempt to define or examine your own status. When you try to define other people's fortunes, for good or ill, inevitably you engage your emotions. But your interpretation satisfies only your imagination, and you are probably wrong. By looking at other people's lives from the outside, only rarely do you see the truth. You do not see how their life is. You see the way you perceive it to be. What you may feel is right for you is wrong for your friend or your neighbour. What you may feel is sufficient and satisfactory would not be sufficient or satisfactory for someone else.

If you let emotions make you feel inadequate you can easily become so. This feeling of inadequacy is insidious; it will become real in all areas of your life. Instead you can become more assertive and strive to rid yourself of any cause to feel inadequate. Your emotions if acknowledged and correctly used will first strive to remove the feeling, and out of your new sense of self-worth, material gain will follow. If, on the other hand, you do not acknowledge your true emotions, but focus directly on material gain without understanding your motivation, you may find that you have suppressed negative feelings which sooner or later will come to the surface.

As one tiny element of one stage of our planet's evolutionary process, you naturally assert your right to exist and to value yourself. Your positive reaction to yourself must never be corrupted by emotions of envy or inferiority. Once you truly value yourself, you will make progress in a rounded, balanced way, with deep understanding of who you are and the power you possess.

Judging emotions

If you start to make judgements about your own emotions, perhaps defining some as valid and some as fruitless, you may be led to think harshly about the emotions and reactions you learned from your family. This will not change anything. If you begin to blame your parents, you have to consider the influence of their parents, which you cannot fully know; and so on and so on back to your distant ancestors in a time and place of which you know nothing.

Consider only your own feelings, and do so with detachment.

You know that powerful, uncertain and mysterious forces may emerge from a mind which is completely dominated by emotions. Such strong feelings may become destructive, and interrupt the natural cycle of your development. Superficially, you recover; but somehow situations, and emotions, and negative consequences recur again and again.

A strong undertow of emotion must at some point be faced and the consequences dealt with. When awareness finally emerges from this kind of self-examination, your duty is to ensure that never again will you destroy yourself, or the world around you, because your emotions are out of control.

There is wisdom to be gained from failure, as there is from success, and it is important to recognise this. If you fail to do so, you will punish yourself with self-loathing and recommence the destructive emotional cycle.

Selfishness

Selfishness lies behind many emotions and if you indulge it you become ill-natured. If you know someone who openly disregards the feelings and rights of others you rightly despise them as selfish; yet selfishness of a kind is what keeps us all alive. You were born with the selfish drive to survive and prosper, but as you go through life you discover that doing so is a question of balance.

If you seize material things from others and then exploit their lack of resources, you unbalance the natural equity of society and promote resentment, retaliation and anarchy. If, on the other hand, you quietly insist that your mind may lead you where it will, and that your thoughts are not bound to any destructive emotions imposed from outside, you retain your own strength of mind and mental health.

Selfishness lies behind greed. The greedy person takes more than their share of resources which are finite, leaving less for everyone else. The greedy person finds that these resources fill the hole where emotional contentment ought to be, and repeats the process; acquisition of resources becomes addictive; it becomes the aim of the greedy person's life, and blunts their human sympathies. Every kind of deceit and backstabbing becomes justified in pursuit of gain. Greed becomes criminal.

Meanwhile no progress is being made. The criminal individual makes no psychological progress, and the disadvantaged majority are crippled by lack of resources and a sense of powerlessness.

Desire

Desire is a kind of magnetism that overwhelms all your other emotions and engulfs the whole of your being. Desire drives you while passion dominates your heart. You find yourself entirely preoccupied: your thoughts are driven by desire, passion, in short by powerful emotions. These feelings, being natural to our make-up on all levels, are clearly innocent, so they captivate you, and trigger your imagination. Your natural drive defines you.

The way you direct your emotions and passions, desires and expectations, may then turn out to imprison you; you place restrictions upon yourself. You refuse to or accept or understand the consequences of such restrictions and you deny that they really exist.

Is it a traditional belief, or a natural law that creates this feeling within you? Are your feelings natural feelings? Because if so you are forced to conclude that they can be detrimental to yourself and destructive. Or perhaps you should question traditional values? Do you fail to understand your own mind, or are you merely afraid of the unknown? Is it natural and right to use your intelligence to create a harmonious social structure?

It is important to visit your mind, and ask these questions, because your mind will respond and the answer will be final.

In your own mind, you must find the true answer. In your own mind, you must identify your realistic aims and ideals, because emotions can affect you negatively, and plunge you deep into darkness for long periods of time.

When you cry out for an answer, what is rightfully yours will be given to you. Your mind is capable of drawing upon all its power and presenting the correct solution at the eleventh hour.

If you mind is supposed to protect you, then it should identify what matters and what doesn't. Allow your mind to choose. Trust your mind to support you as you alter your behaviour, preventing yourself from becoming entrapped by emotionally charged, mistaken actions.

Your decisions are those of your mind; nothing is prevented, but your mind leads you on the true path. You are still free to think as you wish and express yourself as you wish, and this is the ultimate objective and nourishes your creativity.

Fear

The human reaction to fear is to fight or flee. But like most people, you probably lead such a complicated life that your basic responses are dulled; when something frightening rears up ahead, you stand rooted to the spot.

When you feel trapped you clutch at anything you can find, and hang on. Your trepidation runs loose and your imagination magnifies whatever is threatening you. You radiate doubt and uncertainty and refuse to let go of what you have and what you know.

You make no progress. All progress involves risk, and if fear prevents you from taking risks you will be stuck; your hopes become mere wishes, without substance.

Perhaps your fear is a fear of some unknown disease. You have an ache, and can't identify it; you leap to terrifying conclusions based on nothing more than something that happened to someone else, or something you read in the paper. Instead of diagnosing what's wrong, you are displaying an emotional weakness.

Fear must be faced. Confront your fear, and you control your imagination, which is no longer able to magnify the fear. Confronting fear is constructive and quite simple. All you have to do is examine what it is, where it comes from, and separate *realistic* fear from exaggerated emotional panic.

Anger

Anger is always ultimately self-destructive and is usually inspired by fear of the unknown. It is an emotion to be dreaded, since it can so easily spiral out of control. It absorbs far too much of your creativity and imagination, and depresses your general health. You can be literally crippled by it, and your life destroyed.

Throughout history, tribes and factions have felt justified in fighting each other just as individuals have. Although we have evolved into a species of greater intelligence, reaching higher levels of understanding, we still seem unable to stop persecuting our fellow man. Now that only the state has the legal right to express anger through violence, acting in your name, your government will sacrifice your life to achieve material gain or power. And because states command technological powers undreamed of in earlier centuries, the anger of the state can – just like our own personal anger – be so vehement that self-destruction seems preferable to defeat. The results may possibly destroy life on earth.

Anger is the most painful of emotions, and unless conflicts are resolved, the anger they cause will result in self-destruction. The only route to conflict resolution, and dispersal of anger, is spiritual empowerment.

Greed

You've got to speculate to accumulate; no argument there. But there are those who prefer to accumulate not by speculating, but by dominating – in other words by bullying other people: by land-grabbing, theft or cheating. This is greed. These people have no limits to their ambition to dominate and in the worst cases, no limits to how they will keep on accumulating wealth.

They are living in a limited emotional world where everything and everyone has a price – and that's about all.

Take, for example, confidence tricksters. They are extremely good at presenting their case and themselves. They can make most people believe that they are telling the truth. They try to work out what you want to hear. If they can do that, it follows that they could be gainfully employed in trying to provide it; that way they would make both of you happy. Instead they prefer to trick you, steal from you and by so doing make you feel bad about yourself for having been duped. Their motive must be domination; greed is the emotion that drives them, but the wealth itself is of secondary importance except as a status marker.

Envy and arrogance

If, in childhood and adolescence, your material circumstances make you feel excluded from society, you will find life unfair. It is indeed unfair, but that is no reason why you should feel inferior.

A sense of inferiority may make you envious, and you will hurt only yourself. Emotionally, you may feel frustrated by your inability to have and do what more privileged people can. This frustration is negative. The sense of inferiority becomes self-fulfilling. You begin to believe that bad things will always happen to you, and good things won't. Envy puts you in a prison of your own making.

Unless you make a strong mental effort to identify your frustration and force yourself out of the limits it places upon you, you will be dogged by a sense of inferiority for the rest of your days. Avoid envy, which inhibits you, by thinking about the emotions you have, and examining your true mind.

A sense of superiority, on the other hand, will make you arrogant. Arrogance is the obverse of envy. It is an exaggerated sense of entitlement. Only tiny babies are entitled to demand our undivided attention at all times, and even they must quickly learn that their parents have rights too.

If you are lucky enough to have been born with opportunities for a better education and a wider choice of experience, you have no right to consider yourself fundamentally superior to the less privileged multitude.

Arrogance, like envy, is a limiting emotion. It creates resentment, retaliation, criticism and general discomfort, and it cuts you off from experiences that would teach you a lot. There will be things you won't do, as they would conflict with your self-image. When life places you in a situation where you must concede and break these self-limiting restrictions, your body reacts in accordance with your inhibitions. Your emotional 'won't' becomes a physical 'can't'. Your physical movement slows, or maybe you become clumsy or stupid or even self-destructive.

Envy and arrogance inhibit you. Instead, recognise that your fellow human beings belong to your species and your time and are worthy of recognition as individuals. You will find that communicating with them is liberating. Freedom from envy or arrogance gives you confidence. You have personal faults and inadequacies like everyone else, but that is because you are on a journey, and we all address our faults at different stages of life.

Hope

If you allow emotions to drive you, you may find that fear takes over. Unable to face the possibilities ahead, you find you have two options. You may choose to shrink into isolation, as far as possible avoiding communication or physical action, as if life were a storm that must pass over your head; or – and this is the pleasanter option – you may reject unnecessary fear in favour of groundless hope.

You hope you will be safe. You hope against hope that everything will turn out right. What demands you place upon hope! You include in your hopes the whole nexus of circumstances that surround your existence – the environment, the earth, the universe.

Hope is not a strategy. However powerfully you visualise the attainment of your goal, without *action* yours is a futile wish. If you are to ground your hopes in reality, you must take creative action. The first move is yours. All action involves risk, but without risk, there is no hope.

Even if you are blindfolded, sitting in a corner idle, if you are willing to get up and act then true hope will develop. This will not be the kind of groundless wish that is only an escape from fear; it will be a realistic hope, and will bring about changes in your life that you will use on your journey to your goal.

Pride in achievement

Achieve your goal, and you will feel fulfilled and invincible. You know you can accomplish anything; your qualities of leadership emerge; you feel on top of the world and almost indestructible.

Such an extreme of pride may lead you to abuse your new power. You literally have not thought out how to use it wisely. You are secretly aware of this inadequacy and feel insecure. Nonetheless you put your defences up, fearing retribution or revolt; your insecurity makes you suspicious. Now you are behind a barrier, and trapped there. You are unable to see how things really are, and imagine the worst; you do not want anything to change, for any change is a threat.

When, on the other hand, you react calmly to your own well-justified feelings of pride, you do not allow the emotion to overwhelm you. Your defences are not weak, for you have a built-in protective instinct, but you are open to the world and continue your journey while acquiring knowledge, communicating, leading and confidently making changes.

False pride

False pride is not a genuine pride in achievement, but a sham; a platform you construct, and once it is constructed, you believe that you have successfully signalled your superiority to the world, and that the world accepts you at your own valuation.

Be aware of your mood, for it can inspire false pride. If you happen to be feeling compassionate, you will take into account the dilemmas that people have to face and refrain from harsh judgements. But if, for whatever reason, you are in an unsympathetic state of mind, then your judgements will be severe and the door is open for your prejudices to make them more so. At this point the feeling of superiority induced by your transient mood can inspire false pride which will endure.

If some disaster befalls you, false pride is attacked first. You feel diminished as a human being by pain and suffering, or by loss of status or professional disgrace. Until now you have relied on victory over others to support your false pride, but with this disaster you are made weak. You are for once among the losers, and you feel bitter because of the unfairness of it all. You cannot accept that your false pride was a sham, that you can make mistakes and grow old like other people; and you refuse to accept that you are not immune to misfortune or disease. You refuse to accept responsibility for your past, present or future. Your fury is directed outwards into a search for someone to blame.

As the search proves fruitless, your bitterness turns inwards. You become preoccupied with feelings of failure, alternating in some cases with weak attempts to excuse yourself for events, until the whole sorry emotional cycle leaves you depressed and humiliated. With increasing desperation, you hang onto false pride.

Your mind can take no more of this, and there is a physical reaction; you develop a psychosomatic disorder, or several.

Should you feel emotionally defeated by other people? It is far better to concentrate on exercising your own mind and your own abilities, leaving others to do the same. Life should not be approached as a competition. None of us is superior to any other in every respect and none of us can fully understand the depths of another's personality. You cannot, even if you are a judge, know the emotional history of another person or fully understand their motives, especially if their life experience has been very different from yours.

Guilt

Guilt may be justified or not, imposed by others or imposed by ourselves. As with fear and anxiety, it can provoke such inner turmoil that you can't move forward; and as with fear and anxiety, you must confront guilt and deal with it, or the consequences will be disproportionate to the cause, and may manifest themselves physically.

Maybe you feel guilty because you have failed to achieve your own goals. First of all, is this guilt justifiable? Be honest with yourself, for your mind knows the true answer. Did you rely upon hope as a strategy, and fail to apply your mental energy, your physical energy, your capacity for work and your will? If so, there may still be time to clear the decks, get started and recommence your journey.

If circumstances make this impossible, examine your options. Set yourself a different goal. You now know that unless you use all your energy and will, you will not reach this one either. If you are unwilling to make the effort, reject that goal as a possibility, because it too will end in guilt – thereby increasing your burden. This is not such a negative conclusion as it sounds: it is an honest statement that try as you may, you cannot summon up enough interest in the aim to achieve it. You literally don't want it enough.

Consider what you do want. Maybe you want nothing to change. This is nice and comfy, but it is not really an option, is it? Change is inevitable. So choose an aim you *do* have the energy and will to achieve. Draw up a strategy to get there, and set out to complete every stage. You will reach your goal, and as you move forward you will wonder why you ever felt guilty about aspirations that are past, which you were never truly sincere about anyway.

Perhaps you interrogate your mind about these guilty feelings you have and find that they are not justified at all. If so, why have you been feeling them so strongly? Did you make the mistake of bowing to pressure from others? Have negative feelings been projected onto you as a burden? Guilt can be projected, knowingly or unknowingly, not simply by people we know, but by the opinions of society at large. The voices of authority you first heard as a child may resonate in your mind as an adult, and although your reason tells you that what you are doing is personally right and essentially harmless, convention tells you otherwise. If, in these circumstances, you can dismiss your burden of guilt as unjustified, you will help define yourself as the person you truly are.

As a child, you were unduly sensitive to negative thoughts and the negative assumptions of others; as an adult, you are free to reject such implications, and focus on positive thoughts that can transform guilt and weakness to strength and progress.

Your feeling of guilt may be justified because you have caused damage, loss or pain to others. In this case, guilt is the most positive emotion you can have. It is nature's way of telling you to re-examine your motives and re-direct your energies. Think of what you did. What were you aiming to achieve? What emotional need were you trying to satisfy? What was it that made you think that this damaging action was the only way to achieve your goal and make yourself happy? Never be careless, either, of the impact of your *criticism* on another human being. It is too easy to sentence others to darkness, traumas, resentment and rejection.

Unless you can focus on these things, be honest with yourself and make changes in the way you satisfy your emotional needs, the burden of your guilt will remain. You will suppress it but you will remain in turmoil within, and this may cause you to repeat your sterile, guilt-provoking behaviour.

Grief

There is help for grief, but you alone can truly deal with it over the years. What is of concern here is the guilt that sometimes goes hand in hand with it. If the cause is bereavement, irrational guilt can make you as deeply depressed as guilt which is well-founded.

People who have escaped some disaster feel bad because they have survived where others didn't. They know, rationally, that they have no cause for guilt but the emotion is almost too strong for the mind to control. Parents of children who have died suffer perhaps more than anyone, for none of us believe we are going to predecease our children. Parents who have lost a child through miscarriage or termination can torture themselves with the futile, irrational question of self-blame: 'Could I have done something differently?' Their feeling of loss increases and their suffering deepens.

Should you try to suppress these feelings or understand them? You must make the effort to understand, for otherwise you fall prey to long-term depression. Spend time analysing the emotional basis of your thought, and do not presume to think the worst of yourself. Perhaps love and protectiveness, the most wonderful of emotions, are making a martyr of you. Honour the departed by rejoicing in their existence, however brief it was. Remember that this is about their contribution, not about your grief.

Never throw yourself into a vortex of guilt and mental self-torture, for these things lead ultimately to self-pity, which is always dysfunctional.

Anxiety

Of all the emotions that assail you in swift succession throughout your waking hours, one of the least welcome is anxiety. It is the dull child of fear prodded by the imagination. As it gnaws at your unconscious hour after hour, you begin to feel trapped, restricted and unable to apply reason or energy or will to the situation. You are confused, your mind a swirling fog of contradictions. You cannot fight, but nor can you flee: you are stuck. Mentally, you are in a panic.

If you do not deal with anxiety it can drive you to despair and self-destruction: your anxiety makes you your own victim.

Yet it is not difficult to deal with and the sooner you do so, the easier it is.

First distract your consciousness, so that your mind can work in peace to identify the true causes. Concentrate all your energies upon creating a calm space and time in which to bring your deepest thoughts to the surface.

Once you are calm, think: why are you anxious? The root cause may not be what your consciousness tells you. Only your mind will reveal what you are really afraid of. What deep fear has your imagination been working on, that it has created such anxiety? Is it fear of separation, or death, or independence, or loss of approval, or something else?

Is there any factual basis for this fear?

If not, dismiss the anxiety for the minor glitch it is. The situation is just another cycle of life: a mere change, the purpose of which will eventually become apparent. Take action to avoid its negative consequences if you can, but if you cannot, use all your mental energy to figure out how to make the best of those consequences.

If the fear is major, real and unavoidable, then write down what you can do to mitigate its worst effects. *Take action.* Life goes on until the moment of death, and until that moment you are, no matter what your physical disability, active and having an effect in the world. Make it a positive effect.

Anxiety is the least productive, most debilitating of all emotions. Action or acceptance are the only ways to rid yourself of it. Learning to deal constructively with anxiety is excellent training in managing change. Throughout your life you will have to manage change well and calmly, for your own sake and that of those around you. When change is on the horizon, be curious about the conflict between your aims and your fears, and engage the assistance of your mind. Confront anxiety in a spirit of enquiry, for your mind may offer insights that will clarify your future progress or prompt you to investigate new areas of expertise.

Fear of inadequacy

Fear of some personal inadequacy is among the emotions most likely to be suppressed. Many people build careers on expertise that is less than perfect, or make others depend on them when they know that in the final analysis, they will be broken reeds. This kind of suppressed fear of inadequacy is dangerous, because by definition, the person will lose face if it is revealed; they may also fear losing a job, or the trust of someone they love.

In a way they are leading a double life. This shows itself in extremes. Often they tend to be morose, moody, ill-tempered and uncommunicative in private life, while the world thinks of them as sociable high achievers. Alternatively, they are authoritarian: they 'throw their weight about' in an apparent effort to compensate for their metaphorical lack of it. Both these patterns of behaviour are projections of emotional weakness which sooner or later will manifest itself in a physical crisis or compulsive behaviour.

Acknowledge your emotion

Valid emotional outlets like imagination and creativity must be put to work, not stored up without release. Accumulated unacknowledged emotion, positive or negative, can be extremely tiresome and will influence your body as well as your mind. You have to examine and question and negotiate everything that is happening in order to balance and calm your emotions, and be able to deal with matters realistically.

All that you are is filtered through your emotions, everything you perceive has to penetrate the barriers of your emotions and everything that you project from inside has to go through these barriers to be drawn into your mind. There is no 'cure' for emotions; there is only action, and the only valid action is dictated by your mind. Your mind reacts according to your interests, and can see beyond your emotions.

Your emotions can influence your lifespan. Your body is part of all that exists. Like the earth, it possesses depths that are active and at times volatile; and like the planet itself, your living organism can regenerate from within. Be aware that you must do your best to keep your emotions in check. There will be moments when you fail; do not allow your emotions to flood in like a tide and bear you away.

8 Pain, the mind's alarm bell

The susceptible mind

If the mind is so powerful, you may argue, why is it so susceptible to emotion? Why does the mind not intervene more often to prevent you from making destructive emotional decisions?

Sadly, your mind's intervention often goes unrecognised. It comes in the form of pain and weakness in your body. A healthily functioning mind is directed at maintaining a healthy physical organism. Your body is extremely strong and yet fragile; the effect of impact from a fall, or attack by an infection, can literally vary according to your state of mind.

In order to flourish your body requires not only food, air, and water but most importantly, an active mind. The mind organises and analyses your thought processes, the demands of your body, and your emotional implications and influences. This enables it to offer the safest options to the body. In your mind, you weigh all your emotions, memories and physical desires, and the way your mind directs you is always true and unarguable. Confusion is triggered when you ignore your own mind; when you behave according to destructive emotions your mind immediately begins to shut down areas of your body in the hope that it can preserve itself.

The most common form of weakening is self-punishment. This immediately becomes evident as shallow and erratic breathing. Your intake of air is limited, too little oxygen reaches your blood, and your energy is immediately depleted. The simplest way of empowering yourself at moments of weakness is to breathe deeply.

Your mind's next resort is to punish your stomach or your back. Your stomach needs food so that your body can produce energy. When your mind is punishing your refusal to acknowledge its revelations, you suffer loss of appetite, discomfort, even pain.

Without a strong spine, you cannot move. When you act in opposition to the intuition of your mind, your spine becomes painful. Your movement is restricted and you may even become bedridden.

Consciousness to mind to brain

Instructions to the mind are spurred by conscious emotions, translated within the mind and transmitted to the brain. The brain sends impulses to the muscles and organs of the body, and physical reactions take place. For instance if you eat thinking 'I shouldn't be eating this' you'll feel guilt. This guilt remains unresolved, as the will was too weak for the emotion, and a silent instruction passes to the mind. The brain makes the body feel heavy, bloated with guilt. With repeated instances of this behaviour the feeling of heaviness and bloating occurs no matter how insignificant the intake of food. In some cases the body rejects any food at all, so the digestive system falls into turmoil. Now there is real pain, and close family begin to fuss, and imagination takes over. (*What is the matter with me? Is something seriously physically wrong?*) As deterioration persists, the body becomes susceptible to disease.

Self-fulfilling prophecies

Once you are physically weak, you are vulnerable. Those around you are concerned, and make it plain that they are sorry for you. They are unwittingly reinforcing your conviction that your body is at fault, that it is your body that has suddenly collapsed. The solution is available all the time – if only you will interrogate your mind to find it. You don't, because it is easier to react emotionally than to think.

Think about how attitudes towards you, and the attitude to life with which you were brought up, affect you. Because of time and place of your birth and your own nature you may be particularly vulnerable to weakness in certain parts of your body. Or if you are emotional and inclined to worry morbidly about your health, you might say to your family 'I've got swollen glands, and I think I'm coming down with the flu'. With that simple projection of weakness you have instructed your mind that this is likely to happen and now it certainly will happen. The more preoccupied you become the more pain your mind inflicts.

Never ignore chronic pain. It is the mind's alarm bell, a positive thing telling you not to allow your emotions to dominate and lead you in the wrong direction. Instead instruct your mind: *I do not want this.* You are no longer a passive recipient of the mind's frustration: you have stated your willingness to assess your situation, remove emotional obstacles and apply your will to your own recovery.

The healing mind

Although your mind's reaction to undue stress often manifests itself at your weakest moments, at other times you are under stress for a reason. Your mind can tell the difference. You know in your own mind when you are overworking with a productive end in view, or pushing your body to its physical limit for your own goal of self-fulfilment.

It is at moments like these, when you should be as susceptible as the next person to any bug or virus that is going around, that the power of the mind may show itself in constructive action. Perhaps your glands have swollen; you know that it is a warning sign of the onset of a minor illness. If you are aware that everything else in your life is on track, it is highly likely that you can fight off the illness at least temporarily, and insist, successfully, that you will not be unwell at the crucial time.

You are giving your mind the power to reject the illness, and it will respond. Just simple transformative thought will halt the process.

How can this happen? Was the disease imaginary in the first place? It was not, but the most distinguished medical minds in the world are still trying to find out exactly how the mind overcomes illness.

In extreme cases, such as paralysis, the parts of the brain that instruct you to be mobile are unable to connect with limbs and organs via the spinal cord: the connection is physically broken. In theory, the conclusion is obvious, and leads doctors to say things like 'you'll never walk again'. This is a counsel of despair, and is not true. A degree of mobility can be achieved, since with time and hard work, the frailest of connections can be developed. Equally, if your brain itself is damaged your mind is able to seek and find alternative means of operation; so strong is your will, so positive the conviction that *it can be done*, that your brain compensates for its own shortcomings.

These are facts. Nobody knows exactly how it does it, but your mind can triumph over apparently insuperable obstacles. And until someone finds out how to revive lost faculties by means of stem cell treatment, drugs or neurosurgery, your mind – control of your emotions and operation of your will – is your means to achieve health, whether you feel a cold coming on or you have had a life-changing accident. It is your mind that will drive you to exercise, your mind that will kick your immune system into overdrive, and your mind that will use the faculties you have, far beyond a point you would have thought possible.

Once you become aware that your mind is directing you along the correct path, you will not allow emotional stress to dominate your being.

Action

If you wanted to build a house, you'd get some builders to come and start work. If you just kept on thinking about the house, you'd never build it, but would just go on dreaming. In your dreams, as the house began to rise from the ground it would become bigger and ever more more imposing until it towered over the street; then it would get a portico and balconies and a tennis court and some extra floors; and pretty soon it would look like a palace and dominate the city.

Unfortunately, when you have an illness your imagination works the same way. Your headache is magnified into a brain tumour and your tiny zit is probably the start of smallpox, at least. Terror overwhelms your imagination and you feel worse with every minute that passes.

So it is important to inform your imagination that illnesses are not terrifying blots that get bigger, but annoying scratches that your mind can rub out, leaving your body purer than before. Your illness may have become worse because you didn't pay attention to it, but now that you have, it will get better.

If you instruct your mind that you feel ill, and you want comfort, it will tell you to lie down until the weakness passes. But if you instruct your mind that you feel ill, but you want to get better, it will tell you to breathe deeply and concentrate on health, calm and happiness. Your mind is now focussed, and will de-activate negative tensions and activate positive energy to heal you.

9 Instructing your mind

Know your own mind

Be prepared to be amazed. Your mind is wonderful. The more familiar you become with its wonders the more you will appreciate the tremendous power that lies within you and the more exhilarated and positive you will feel.

As you journey through life, you owe it to yourself to use the full capacity of your mind, so that your life is shaped according to your mind's design. When you think, you begin to see your life from afar, and appreciate your situation dispassionately. When you imagine, you reach a state of mind that is outside your normal emotional consciousness; a state that is true and emanates from a spirit beyond yourself.

The purpose and direction of your life become clear when you enter this spiritual state. You seem to be at one with a superior intelligence, one that is eternal and will be reborn.

Until now you have been aware of your five senses; yet you find that there are others. Once you know your own mind, you will find that previously hidden senses and sources of energy are available to you. One is the power to instruct your mind.

Your mind's deeper functions are simply related and connected to the wisdom of nature, and as it gathers knowledge on your journey through time and space, your mind evolves. Deep within its memory are keys to rebuilding the parts of your body that need attention. As this healing proceeds, all emotion is shed. Your mind senses communication from your every nerve, and works with what your body offers. When you open communication and instruct your mind to make you healthier and stronger in mind and body, you will understand still more how the slightest emotional intervention can upset your mind's delicate balace.

Reject malign emotions

Of these the greatest is fear. You wish other people health, wealth and happiness and want these things for yourself; yet too often you may find yourself in an anxiety state because you have been told that you should expect to be ill, poor and unhappy.

Instruct your mind to reject fear.

Most people live in fear. Maybe the spread of fear best serves those who claim knowledge and superiority above us all – be it the supplier of our food, the dictator of our laws or the provider of our medication. You are well until you are trapped by some physical ailment, and from that moment on your life belongs to others.

Avoid over-indulgence, so that your body can cope and maintain its natural healthy balance. Allow your mind to create balance in your thoughts, and do not focus on emotional issues.

Sometimes people fear change. But change is, of course, a constant; it is a phenomenon of which we are all part and on which we all depend. Just imagine that today repeated itself today and tomorrow and the day after that; imagine you never felt any emotional change and never aged. You would create nothing new; you would not change, or evolve; you would be less dynamic than a rock. The earth itself is depends on the pull of exterior forces to maintain its rotation, and cannot change to benefit life unless its rotation continues.

Change is important: it is a natural life force. Be open to it whatever it may bring, for even depression and frustration and sadness are emotions you can learn from, so long as you use your mind to analyse these things and guide you through.

Understand your mind

Your mind is naturally positive and forward-thinking. How did you learn to walk and talk as a baby? You learned because you expected to. And because everyone learns, no-one saw you wobbling and burbling and falling over and decided you were destined to fail. They encouraged you because they knew you had an end in mind and however long it took, and however often you fell over or said Ga-Goo instead of 'Mama', you'd walk and talk in due course. And once you learned to walk and talk, you learned other things by experience. You didn't put your hand in a flame, you didn't walk into the road without looking. These things took more guidance from others, but in the course of time they too became second nature to you, as everyone expected they would. Nobody said 'you can't.' Everyone knew you would learn from your physical experiences because that is how your mind works.

However, your mind can imprint troubled or negative messages. In unusual circumstances natural fear and distress may have proved overwhelming. Afterwards, memories will trigger these negative emotions – often when the fear or distress no longer serve a purpose. If this is the case your mind must be instructed not to replay this cycle, for it damages you.

The mimicking reflex

From birth, you learned by imitation. Adults expected you to react to smiles and frowns and gentle noises, and you did; at first you were puzzled and just gurgled or cried but soon you began to watch carefully and mimic exactly. People in a family imitate each other unconsciously, without intention. Spiritual connections are strongest where this happens.

Small children mimic unconsciously. If a baby touches another baby's face, the second baby usually does the same in return. If a quiet child spends time in a room with a hyperactive child, when the quiet one returns to his own environment he will start to copy what he has seen. If he gets the attention he is looking for, he may persist in this kind of behaviour. It is out of character, but the attention he gets makes it worth the trouble.

As you grow up, you begin to identify with others. You start by putting yourself into the mind of a hero in a story; you are scared when he is in danger and exultant when he triumphs. This makes you feel free. You begin to mimic the behaviour of people you admire in real life. If you gain approval, other people will copy you.

The behaviour you imitate is a reflection of your emotional state at the time. You may mimic strength or weakness, mental or physical characteristics. If these states are out of character, you may be forced into situations which confuse you; you won't have the natural resources to deal with them.

Adults, like small children, will alter their behaviour to get approval or attention. This new, self-imposed behaviour can become such a powerful element of your interaction with other people that without it you are lost. You learn to act out certain patterns in all situations, without thinking. You lose your identity and don't know how to deal with yourself any more.

Your identity has become corrupted in an effort to make yourself feel good, but this corruption runs deep and is hard to unpick; who are you really? Who were you, before you began to pretend?

If you are to be conscious of your own tendency to imitative behaviour, and control it, you must focus on it. and monitor the way you behave. Perhaps you find yourself saying or doing something because people you admire behave that way. But the attitudes and behaviour of those people may place them in situations you're not equipped to deal with. Remember that you are unique. Don't lose sight of your natural personality and your own strengths. Project calm and effective energy, and allow others to do the same.

The search for approval

We often imitate people because we want to be like them, and we want to be like them so that they approve of us. Imitative behaviour is not necessarily negative; to some extent the social structure requires it. At one extreme it ties you down to a restricted range of behaviours, and at the other it makes you reject the importance of others' approval altogether. Neither extreme is desirable.

At school you sought approval from your teachers, but also endorsement by your peers. You had to fit in in order to survive. If you didn't, you would be isolated. Yet conforming to the group may have harmed your school career and even your adult life. If you suppressed your real self, you may still be tense and unhappy and not as successful as you could be, but what was the alternative? You did not want be the left-out child, stuck on the sidelines, unable to participate or be accepted, the one who was ridiculed, isolated or even bullied.

Send your own children to a school that lets them express themselves, that encourages them learn where their talents lie and what the fundamental issues of life are; a school that respects them as unique individuals.

Remember that while your perceptions of others, and their perceptions of you, may change, you will stay fundamentally the same. You need not look for status approval but only for self-confidence, born out of understanding and self-respect. There will be times when you sacrifice your imagination, curb your freedom and change your behaviour – all in order to reach an objective. You feel drawn to achieve a higher status regardless of the consequences, knowing that if you don't sacrifice something of yourself, you will not obtain the approval that enables you to move forward.

If this is your dilemma, do not allow your drive to succeed to blind you to who you really are. Insincere actions and behaviour may have long-term consequences. It is better, whenever you can, to use your creativity and freedom to follow your own path. Otherwise you will be forever seeking the approval of others and will live in support of their view of the world, which is not yours.

From babyhood you are brought up to take notice of the encouragement or disapproval of your elders. Later on, this familiar human interaction can reinforce an inferior position (as an approval-seeker) or a superior one (as one who demands satisfaction). Those who are 'demanding' may misuse their demands by inflicting them on others, in other words by misusing power to enforce a relationship of superiority.

If your intentions are clear and will not harm anyone, you will have no need to give or seek approval. Your thoughts and beliefs require freedom of expression, and in the nature of things will capture the attention of some and not others. Those who are not interested will have no bearing on your life, and those who are, will contribute to your developing thoughts. Be true to yourself above all, so that you can give of yourself.

Know when to move on

You grow upwards and move *forwards*. You have to make a conscious effort to walk backwards or sideways and even then, if you don't look carefully and move slowly you'll run into an obstacle. Nature tells you to look and walk forward.

In life, you cannot move back through time, and if you try to look backwards as you move inexorably forward, you will make slow, uncertain progress. If you constantly look back on your life, you detach yourself from the demands of the present moment, which will never come again.

Over-involvement with your memories is a trap. Perhaps you feel that the emotions of the past are unresolved; that a deep trauma is not healed. But you must instruct your mind to understand that the cycles of the past have been completed and can never be altered to suit your own needs and desires. Traumas, like wounds, heal best in their own natural time.

Perhaps you are beset by indecision. You cannot separate your emotion (often fear) from your mind's better judgement. This is a denial of life. If you are in search of answers, try to search with resolution, for indecision can suck you down like quicksand, and stagnant thoughts are poisons.

Take action. Write down on paper the people involved, the issues involved, and the fears you have.

Are your fears real or 'imaginary', that is, real but highly unlikely?

What is the worst thing that could happen? How would you deal with that? (The fact is, you would deal with it, because you are strong and a natural survivor.)

What is the best thing that could happen? How likely is it to happen? Are there actions you must take to make it happen? Are you truly willing to focus and commit to it?

What does your mind tell you?

Focus

Instruct your mind to keep focussed on the present moment. You will need to think and question all the time. Make the effort. When events begin to shape themselves without major hindrance you will know you are on the right track; if, on the other hand, what is happening makes you feel uneasy, your emotions have interfered. Your emotions are probably telling you to pursue an inner desire rather than a logical thought. Apply your mind to the issue.

Learning to focus requires determination, effort and staying power. Write down your thoughts on paper. Decide what you want, and why; what is going wrong, and why. Examine your conclusions. Where do emotions intervene? Whose emotions? Are these useful and valid emotions? This becomes a form of acknowledgement to your mind, which calms you as you begin to assess the options and focus on the solution.

In the course of every cycle, you need to draw upon your mind for insight. Even when you are making emotional choices you should maintain contact with your mind. Once your mind drives the changes in your life, the cycles become positive and progressive, and you go smoothly forward.

Be prepared

If your opportunities are to be realised, you need to be vigilant, shrewd and accepting of the inevitable. It is important to understand that the regular cycle of life may be overthrown at a moment's notice, and a new one take its place. If this kind of unplanned, probably unwelcome change happens to you, you must accept it in both its aspects: the ending of one cycle and the beginning of another. This important talent for *acceptance* will help you harness your emotions and translate them positively into endurance and patience.

As your life's current cycle is transformed into a new one, perhaps all you have left of your old life is memories – and your capacity to think. At this time, your intelligence will tell you that radical life changes are bound to create stress and sometimes fear. Your comfortable existence becomes full of uncertainties and you feel overwhelmed by the unknown. As you are driven to change you face new kinds of challenge; but new kinds of elation will be yours when you meet and overcome these challenges.

At some point in your life, your material status may change for better or worse. Be certain that there are important lessons to be learned, and it is only by accepting and embracing change that you can respect this as a necessary cycle in your progress. If your material status is firmly established in your mind's eye, so long as you take appropriate action you will attain that status.

Perhaps you are working steadily towards achieving a goal. If so don't forget that the goal simply represents the end of one cycle and the beginning of another. Nothing is forever; everything changes, except the mind and spirit which drive you, and are eternal.

10 Regeneration

Having a baby

When you are nine months pregnant and your labour pains begin, you understand the inevitability of it all. This hurts, but *there is no way back*. Just like your baby, you can only go forward. So you may as well make this as positive and painless an experience as you can – and remember the joyous reward that will make it all worth while.

Don't assume that you must have drugs or surgery. Unless a complication arises that may be harmful to you or your baby, you shouldn't even think about surgery. A natural birth is a liberating experience that helps tremendously in understanding about yourself, your capabilities and your duties as a mother.

Focussed breathing is a skill most women learn in pregnancy, but it will help you throughout your life.

Focus on your mind and keep your focus there.

During your contractions, breathe slowly *in* through your mouth and *out* through your nose, as deeply as you can, thinking about the oxygen that is going to help your baby.

As the birth approaches, breathe deeply and slowly *in* through your nose and *out* through your mouth.

Infertility

The birth of a new human being is the most wonderful experience you ever have; a new spirit comes from nowhere into the real world. And because your deepest, most emotionally stirring perceptions are connected with the *spiritual* importance of a birth, your barely acknowledged tension and fear of such a possibility can make your body, male or female, resistant to the possibility of impregnation.

If you think that you may be infertile, practise relaxation techniques. This will calm your mind, and you will no longer think of yourself as 'trying' to have a baby, which is not something an adult human being should ever do. If you are of child-bearing age and there is nothing physically wrong with either of you, then intercourse will sooner or later result in pregnancy.

Don't overlook the fact that your own development should be mature if you're to acquire what is rightfully a duty for life. If you're not ready for the responsibilities of parenthood, your body may resist. You need spiritual maturity to be the guardian of another spirit.

Alternatively, you may feel anxious; you are afraid for whatever reason that what you most want isn't going to happen. This can be a self-fulfilling prophecy.

Ask yourself why you have these emotions. There are probably a whole collection of personal and cultural reasons.

If you have experienced the sadness and trauma of miscarriage, this can understandably make anxiety an obstacle to conception. But it is an anxiety that can be dealt with. If there is no physical reason why you should not conceive, then you will, and with appropriate medical advice you will carry the baby to term. A change of attitude is very important; there should be no anxiety, but a fresh, calm, positive outlook.

Perhaps, on the other hand, you are unconsciously reluctant to be pregnant. You are afraid of looking like a skittle and being sick all the time. But it's not quite like that. Most women feel perfectly fine, in fact fantastic, for the whole nine months and everyone who sees you knows that your bulbous new silhouette is only temporary.

Maybe it's the responsibilities and restrictions of parenthood that you dread. It's true, parenthood does entail a radical re-think of your identity. But did you really intend to be a hip'n'happening young singleton at forty or fifty? Perhaps not. There comes a time when parental responsibilities are the challenge you most want. As for restrictions, for every club you no longer have the energy to go to, there's an excuse to have dinner at home with people you really like and want to see; for every day you would have spent in lonely contemplation of your own navel, there's a fresh magical moment in your child's development to watch and rejoice in.

Maybe the birth is what you're scared of. This is pointless. We have evolved over millions of years to do it this way.

If, as a woman, you want a child, this is the deal: it hurts intermittently for a while, then a lot and almost constantly for a few hours, and then it's over, and the baby has arrived and everybody's ecstatic.

All this takes place in the course of a day or two, which in the great scheme of things isn't long. If it were worse, nobody would ever have a second, third or seventeenth child; yet they do. The pain is time-delimited.

It is also natural; it's not a sign of illness, any more than getting bigger is, or getting the baby blues or having morning sickness. All these things are part of the nine-month event. On the day, most births are routine and without complications, and if your baby's birth gives no cause for concern there is little point in demanding drugs to get you through it. The birth is about the baby, not you, and you really don't have an excuse for inflicting any possible chemical side-effects on this little mite at the moment he or she comes into the world.

Put your groundless fears into proportion (they are fears, after all; they are not real).

The next generation

When you decide to have children you do so in the understanding that you will have to make sacrifices. You may normally sacrifice your own energies to create something or acquire a skill, but your ultimate creative achievement is your children; it is your children whose balance and intelligence will be handed down to future generations.

Life begins at the moment of conception with one birth and many deaths, as millions of sperm die and just one combines with the genetic material of the mother to form the foetus. As soon as this new life has begun to develop in the womb, it is influenced by the mother's environment. If she is under stress the baby may be affected by chemical or hormonal changes in her body. When she is perturbed or calm, miserable or ecstatic, angry or in a fit of the giggles, the substances released in her brain will affect the growing child for good or ill. And as hearing develops the baby may be subject to the effects of soothing music or sharp, loud noise. The physiological effects of these, too, upon the mother will affect the child in the womb.

These emotional stresses and floods of feeling register with the child's mind, which naturally seeks balance; extremes are not beneficial. The slightest build-up of tension within the body can influence the flow of energy to the foetus. The unconscious mind of the unborn child registers the tension and reacts with the instinctive negative or positive response it will later show in life.

All this goes on out of sight in the course of a pregnancy as the child's mind and spirit – the 'personality' that makes it unique from birth – are mysteriously formed. As a parent, it will be your pleasure to watch and listen as this personality emerges from babyhood; and your duty to guide, but never to stifle it.

The fragile personality

Consider what is really suitable for children and young people, having respect to their unique personalities. Ask yourself about the attitudes with which you bring up your own children, and whether or not your attitudes ultimately benefit you, or your child, or both, or neither of you.

Perhaps you have incited your child to do what you want with a threat or a reward. And perhaps the idea backfired, and you recognised that your threat was blackmail and your reward a bribe. There was some short-term benefit to you, but your children did not understand what they were being asked to do, or feel true interest or enthusiasm; they were simply responding to a stimulus.

Recognise, also, emotional blackmail, of which the cruellest kind is the threatened withdrawal of love or respect, followed by the parent's decline into illness or worse. Adult children recognise this for what it is, but small ones feel bottomless guilt and some never recover. Emotional blackmail can result only in despair for both parties.

Blackmail and bribery will never work. Your task as the elder person is to inspire the young to freedom of thought and expression and assist in their progress. Your children need constant nurturing to release their imagination, their creativity, and their capacity for hard work and fortitude in pursuit of their goals. Your reward is priceless: a happy relationship with your children at all ages.

Your suggestions will affect their behaviour throughout their lives. Let these suggestions be empowering, rather than weakening. Praise their smallest achievement. The emotions of children are vulnerable and enduring; a lifetime of positive exchanges, constructive criticism and useful advice can be undermined by one disparaging remark. If you have a tendency to sneer, to be spiteful or sarcastic, curb your tongue when you have children.

Understand that the aspect of their behaviour you find most

worrying is likely to be a weakness of your own. This is not to say it may not be a weakness of theirs too, but simply to remind you that as you guide your children away from the pitfalls, do not allow your emotions to make you over-react.

From their first decade, children are finding out what fascinates them and what doesn't, what they want to pursue and what they don't. Too often, older people thoughtlessly create limitations in the minds of children at this stage. The environment itself appears to present indomitable obstacles, usually material ones, as children learn to place themselves and you in the social hierarchy of privilege. Do not reinforce disadvantage by denying the possibility of *change through focussed work.* Do not pass on your own fears or perceived inadequacies. Do not judge them. Let them find their own limits. Every moment is vivid and new and challenging for them; let them accumulate a mountain of small triumphs.

When they begin their second decade in life, they start to grow away from you, and their behaviour alters. You will understand this and be prepared for it. You have to lose control in some respects, and there is no need for resentment. They will naturally reject some aspects of your outlook and your life, for this is part of the normal cycle that allows them to become fully independent of you in due course.

But what if their drive away from you leads them into danger as adolescents? Observe and listen closely, and above all keep your channels of communication open. Their bodies are transforming themselves and their emotions are volatile. Often teenagers develop psychosomatic illnesses because they are overwhelmed by a storm of new emotions and passions and awakening sexuality. They are learning to deal with new freedoms, and while you know they have not experienced much yet, in their own minds they understand the world better than you and are almost certainly capable of improving on your efforts.

It is important to respect the young, to support their endeavours and to care enough to allow them to grow away from you without undue conflict. Above all, never make them feel powerless or unwanted. Their own imagination and talent will transform them into the people they want to be, and if their self-confidence and self-expression have been allowed to grow strong, the human race will speed along the path to a better future.

They will never forget their parents; they will carry through life your warnings and encouragement, as well as the genes which provided them with the energy, strength and creativity to pursue their own path.

Perhaps you rebelled against one parent or both. You may still disagree with them about nearly everything, but when you have children of your own, you will almost inevitably find yourself saying the things they said to you and even behaving in the same way towards your children; for parenthood, too, is a cycle within your life, with its own beginning and end, and you imitate the behaviour you know best.

To your parents, you are always a daughter or a son. Even if your achievements far exceed theirs, when you are 80 and they are 100, you will still in some fundamental way defer to them as unique influences in your life. It will be the same for your own children.

Expectations

You have no right to expect sacrifices from your children, but you must always be prepared to make sacrifices for their sake. You are older, but from the moment of their birth the future rests with them, and it is your responsibility to be aware of their needs at all times, and to give them some guidance that may help them through life.

Other animals naturally assist their children, and do not expect their children to do anything for them in return. Yet human beings often place huge emotional demands upon their offspring. Sometimes wishful thinking makes a parent identify a child as uniquely talented and push them to achieve, telling them that this is the way they will become rich and famous. Depending on the field of endeavour, this kind of brainwashing will have one or other kind of negative effect. If the child is driven to exhaustion, the effect is resentment. If the child is spoiled by unrealistic praise, he or she will become idle and arrogant.

Of course your children are the smartest and most beautiful in the world, but when you are tense and criticise, it is really their innocence that you find inadequate. At such moments their future can be driven in the wrong direction by parental force. Education is a gift, not some kind of signal to satisfy the parent's imaginary critics. The warnings and demands of a parent, which sons and daughters will hear in their heads far into adulthood, can be so strong as to curb their individuality. Too strong a will, applied to the direction of a sensitive child, may be the product of an inflated ego. Suppressing the child's creativity, emotion, desire, call it what you will, this deliberate sealing-off of the child's *mind* will cause troubles in later life. There will be chronic physical troubles, but also an obvious mismatch between the person and the life they are leading.

Often parents adhere to religious and social beliefs which are inappropriate to the time and place. Repressive ideas may be dictated by a minority within a community, while the majority dare not rebel. There are elders who have never learned to learn from experience, since they themselves were forced to accept dogma from their elders. They will deny that their rules may be inadequate or morally questionable, because they have lived their lives by them. Confronting the fact that their own minds were stifled in childhood will undermine the way they have lived ever since. Instead, blindly and callously they inflict their rules on the next generation.

In a situation like this, the whole community infantilises the questioning young person; not simply is there one autocratic adult to deal with, but a whole phalanx of parents, priests, institutional disapproval and sometimes even the law behind them. What young person can withstand such pressure? Where inappropriate values are imposed on individuals with this kind of force, they must live in denial of their own resentment. This may find release in retaliation against society outside the repressive group or in some form of self-destruction. Anger will inevitably be released as aggression.

Control

You may be someone who likes to be in control. This is healthy: it is good to be in control of yourself, your own time and your own environment; by taking control of your life you feel that you can live in harmony with the tangible world.

But you assert control over others only to satisfy your ego, which is the platform from which you present yourself to the world – and to your children. Control can become power, and power can be misused.

The wisest advice is: *Do not impose your will upon others and do not allow others to impose their will upon you.* This applies in all areas of life. It applies between family and friends, colleagues at work and in all that you do. So long as you avoid placing demands and burdens upon other people, or expecting them to comply with your desires, you owe them nothing; they cannot legitimately expect you to do their bidding.

Never feel the need to impress to win people over. Just do your best, and rely on your own merits and spiritual force, which will be recognised by those who themselves are worthy of recognition.

You are equal to others in all you do. The only authority you possess is your unique mind. Your mind requires freedom to guide you along your journey. No single moment is quite like any other, and your free mind will be alert enough to learn something new from every moment through which you live.

If there were no elders or authorities, and no-one you consider superior in any way, would you need to seek someone's approval, or would you be free? It may be hard to imagine life without conformity in some degree; when you were a child, it was natural to seek the approval of those who were older and knew more. Yet to do this as an adult is to seek to fulfil the dreams and wishes of others, and it limits your own dreams and wishes. If you seek approval from people who consider themselves more powerful or knowledgeable than you, they will argue strongly that your position is wrong. They will seek to undermine you, minimise your talents and make you feel inferior. Do not let this happen.

It is hard not to feel in awe of some people, for you are brought up to respect figures of authority. By implication you will seek their approval: you will try to make a good impression in order to be accepted. You become over-confident, or shy, or nervous – all behaviours which indicate that you are suppressing your natural self.

Yet suppose you don't suppress your natural self. Suppose you behave as you wish to. Do you feel a twinge of guilt? It would be natural enough, since you are conditioned to suppress your feelings in the presence of your social or intellectual superiors. Your mind tells you you have done nothing wrong, but emotionally you suffer from a niggling fear that you have failed in some small, significant respect that you cannot quite identify. Do not allow guilt to make you timid, for it comes from the past, and is now redundant. If your intentions are clear and pure, you have every right to express your own feelings.

Those who continually seek the approval of their parents never own their own lives. Make every effort to distance yourself, for no parent has any right to burden their offspring with damaging guilt. Nor does any child have the right to make a parent feel guilty

Breaking the cycle

Sometimes rebellion takes the form of an inner conviction that important tasks lie ahead. If you are such a rebellious child, you may have set off on a lonely journey, in which you were alienated not only from the ideas you were brought up with, but from society itself. Had you been supported in your endeavour to know your own mind (supported, that is, by a parent's respect) you would have been able to use your mind's wisdom for good from the start.

The drive within is dynamic and begins with acknowledgement of your mind's power and validity. Once your mind is your acknowledged master, you can mentally travel back in time through the cycles of your life to understand the advice and rules you have been expected to live by. Allow your mind to choose which of them is right for you, and which you instinctively reject. Make your peace with the past. Free yourself from the restrictions and inner messages which have been imposed from outside, and which have hindered you. They may come unbidden into your consciousness for many years before they finally fade, but you must reject them if you are to find your own way to change.

As you detach your emotions from the confused turmoil of the past, you may need to detach yourself for some time from your parents. You must be free to examine new ways, and so long as your intentions are honourable there should be no guilt about doing so.

If you are a parent you may wish to release your children from the restrictions of your creed or social group, while retaining the discipline necessary for their young minds to flourish. Give them the self-confidence to pursue their own interests in a constructive way, though hard work and creative endeavour and respect for those of your traditions which calm and benefit them.

Should they ever recognise that they are on a false path, they must have the strength to stop and re-direct their energies at once. None of us is conclusively aware of what lies ahead. Lives can be turned upside down in a moment, without warning. Let your children have no cause to regret wasted time.

Reconciliation

Just as the child inevitably strikes out on its own, it is almost inevitable that conflict takes place and reconciliation follows. When you find yourself in this situation as a child or a parent, don't leave it to the other side to do all the work. Reconciliation is a restoration of balance. It means accepting that now, as independent entities, you can co-exist in affectionate acceptance of one another's past emotions and respect for the sanctity of their present views; life, for all parties, has moved on. You can never forget but you can forgive. The parent, as the older party to whom deference is naturally due, must begin the process of reconciliation.

And what if you fail to achieve a reconciliation? Never give up hope, but remember that change represents an energy that drives you forward. Brooding over the past will only cause depression. If you and your children are thoughtful and self-sufficient, then in due course both parent and child will recognise what the other represents, and value it, rather than blaming them for what (in the other's opinion) they should be.

11 The search for identity

Ancestors

However decisively you separate yourself from your parents, you remain influenced by the fact of their existence. You are the product of their union: this will never change. Yet if you question the way they look and speak and think and behave, you may feel so alienated that you wonder whether they can really be related to you at all.

This is where the search for identity begins. Mystified by your living family and the random fact of your having been born into it, you may be among the thousands who feel compelled to find out more about their grandparents, great-grandparents and so on back into the umpteenth generation. Is this simply an interest in history? Maybe it is, but maybe you are also seeking the roots of your own personality and talents and enthusiasms; or maybe you know the kind of person you would like to be, and are searching your family history for the person you believe you *ought* to be.

Yet your identity is within you, here and now. The only place your search needs to start is with yourself. Analyse your emotions and whether or not they are useful to you, and don't keep looking back at your ancestry or your childhood. What is past links you to your future, but need not, and must not, dictate your future.

There is no point in telling yourself that if this or that had not been the case, life would have been better, or different. If you look behind you become too absorbed to look ahead. However hard you peer into the past, you can never get it into sharp focus. Besides, you are only an observer and your point of view is one of an infinite number. Instead be grateful that you come from a long line of survivors, and look ahead. The stage on which you must play your part is here and now.

Categories

Perhaps, like most people, when you meet a disabled person the encounter occupies your thoughts more than it would were the person able-bodied. Most people who meet the disabled come away feeling sorrow and pity, as well as both superiority (because they have the good fortune not to suffer like that) and inferiority (because if they did suffer, they don't think they'd have such fortitude).

These confused reactions emerge because you have an image of perfection; an image of what the ideal should be, in appearance, character, voice, manner and everything else. You're never completely satisfied that you or anyone else matches up to this, but there it is: the ideal. Against it you measure yourself and everyone you care about, approving of this aspect and disapproving of that. And you raise barriers to protect your own status by disapproving of the categories into which other people fall.

This habit of categorising *by preference* is one that most of us apply to all areas of our lives. If you recognise the tendency in yourself, you will also know that it often leads you to be prejudiced against the slightest deviation from the preferences by which you define yourself. The deviation may be anything, from the colour of a shirt along a scale of importance that rises all the way to belief in a religion. All you know is, you don't think much of it, it's not your kind of thing, and you don't particularly want to have anything to do with people who wear that kind of shirt or subscribe to that religion. This, of course, creates barriers for you, as well those individuals against whom your prejudices are directed.

These barriers are unnecessary. Judgements by prejudice are redundant. If your identity is strong you do not need them and must make every effort to clear them from your thoughts. Drop your guard, and you will start to learn more from all that is around you. Only when you are free of this tendency to put everything into categories will others be free to impress you to their full capacity. Instead of judging, be curious: you will find that you are able to create a kind of support and unity that is productive and free from prejudice.

Or perhaps you know people who seem interesting and perhaps in some way able to reach the ideal. And you begin to fantasise; you are consumed by an imaginary idealised vision of someone else's life, and forget to pay attention to your own. You almost start to believe it's you, not the other person, who's living their life. You are absorbed by something that is not within your control, and this is not the way things are meant to be; you are supposed to be living your own life, not concentrating on someone else's. But you start to try directing this other person's life in the way you think will help it approach your ideal.

This is impossible. It will make you both discontented. You fail to manipulate the other person, and start to feel frustrated by failure. Frustration can dominate you, and spiral out of control.

Perhaps there is something in the life of those you try to manipulate that you really want; a way you want to be. It is connected with the universal tendency to imitate those whose values or appearance or lifestyle seem desirable. But once the honeymoon period is over, you have to revert to your own needs and demands. Remember that your identity is unique; you cannot take over someone else's, and you have no authority to impose values or behaviour on other people's lives.

The seasons

Your identity springs from the rhythms of nature.

Spring

If you are born in spring your imagination will be stimulated by the colours of emergent life around you. The flowers are beginning to open and the sky is blue. You want to know whether the colour of the petals will be vivid and true, whether the flower will survive, or whether it will tilt and fall; this sense is mirrored in your own feeling about yourself. Your projection of yourself is as colourful, as fragrant and as strong as a flower, but your emotions focus on what your weaknesses are and how you will be judged. If at some point you feel inadequate or belittled, your past failures overwhelm you and you either fall apart or become aggressive. You are constantly in an emotional cycle in which you calculate your own status in relation to other people and your own ideas in relation to other ideas; you are uncertain of what is right, and what is wrong. If you were a flower, your stem would be weakening, and your unopened bud would hesitate to open, uncertain of its natural beauty, colour and scent. A closed bud remains remains small, weak and pathetic.

If you use your imagination you can project yourself differently. Use it to create in yourself all the the vivacity, beauty and strength that will capture the attention of those around you. Your power lies in the limitless spectrum available to you: your creativity is drawn to what is vivid and all you think and do and write is expressed through your visual, emotional imagination. Experiment with the colours that surround you, which can change your mood.

Summer

If you are born in the heat of the summer you will suffer extremes. The heat can burn and dehydrate you, but the barren autumn lies beyond. You will battle with insecurity; you will forever be worrying about the lean times that may lie ahead, and making forecasts about what may happen. If this is done in a negative spirit, your own spirit will be negative whether or not the worst happens. Self-punishment is the companion of guilt, which only increases your insecurity and weakness. This can affect you physically, unless you project your negative feelings into your consciousness and decide to transform them.

Positive thoughts are more rewarding than negative ones. Remember that the autumn's decline, and winter's hibernation, strengthen life for the spring and summer to come. Learn to identify each obstacle whose shadow you see ahead, and transform it into an opportunity. Your doubt will be transformed into certainty about your destiny.

Autumn

If you are born in the autumn life is shutting down around you, and you must wait a long time, doing little, before spring arrives. This saps your will. You seem relaxed and carefree because there is plenty of time to imagine and dream about the future but you feel even that is pointless. Hibernation is ahead so you won't be able to act anyway.

Then you feel guilty, and guilt is an emotion strong enough to cause your body to shut down, along with your will. However, if you take control you will recognise the value of time. The approach of winter gives you time to master issues that challenge your mind and body, time to learn to follow instructions, and time to investigate the possibilities dormant in your own mind.

Winter

Winter brings hibernation. Animals store their energy and wait for the spring to arrive. Although a hibernating animal is asleep, connections between body and brain are not severed; its mind is active and aware and the functions of its body simply slow down.

If you were born in winter, you will communicate easily

with your unconscious mind. You are creative and naturally sensitive and aware. Sometimes you may struggle as the speed of your mind isn't matched by your body. Your imagination zips from one thing to another, you can't keep up, and you can't resolve your own impulses and unresolved thoughts. This can make you look for ways to escape. You are really trying to escape the turmoil within.

Yet since you can communicate on a profound level with your unconscious mind, you can instruct it. Only learn to organise your thoughts and project them constructively and you will achieve balance and start to move forward in your life.

Your own cycles of life

As a child you were full of wonder about the marvels and possibilities of the world around you; as an adolescent, you learned to move on, to strike out on your own, to take your own risks, make your own mistakes and win your own battles.

We may generalise about the natural cycles of life. There is no firm rule, but it is usually in your third decade, your twenties, that you test and exercise all the things you have learned in childhood and adolescence. As you implement new skills and explore new ideas you will have to be assertive. If you understand your own mind, you will drive yourself in the right direction. You will not allow yourself to be pushed into areas of endeavour that you find essentially uninteresting or unsympathetic. If you do, you will learn too well the sense of inadequacy and disillusionment that comes of having tried to live up to somebody else's expectations.

In thirties, you use the skills and experience you have gained to capture the position you were aiming for. This is a key decade, for besides drawing on your physical energy you will need all your mental and emotional energy to achieve as much as you possibly can.

As you enter your forties you become strongly conscious that your time on earth is finite, and begin to ask yourself whether your life has been a success or a failure. Are you on the right track? Have things turned out the way you hoped? These are the thoughts that become dominant. You may at this stage become critical of everything in your life. You may begin to slow down; you get restless, but at the same time you feel you must create security. Your working and social life become structured and always purposeful; inwardly you feel every minute counts. Perhaps you sense that your days are numbered, and where changes are necessary they must take place without delay.

This is the age of the mid-life crisis. There is a popular belief that some emotional crisis takes place at this time and that you, in your forties, will be vulnerable. You may have an image of yourself at some peak state, from which the only way is down. It is important to recognise that this peak state exists only in your imagination. It is equally possible to take the optimistic view that your second stage is the stage when you will achieve most and be able to build upon all the gains and insights of your earlier years.

Old age

The prospect of ageing may daunt you, and if so you may in middle life make changes in your lifestyle and habits to delay the ageing process. If you try to turn back the clock and ignore the passage of years, you will be forced to confront the fact that you are growing older; if you do not think about it or talk about it, certainly others will and they will draw your attention to the fact.

None of this matters once you accept that new doors can open at any stage in life. All you have to do is keep moving forward, never getting stuck in the past or in an outdated, inappropriate image of yourself. The past will serve its purpose automatically; you do not need to interrogate it for answers; its wisdom will spring to mind when it is required. Always be prepared for change, and seek the strength of your mind to help you exploit whatever opportunities come your way.

An active mind is a healthy mind and reaching retirement age does not mean you opt out and resign your future to fate. As an older person, it is vital that you should be active and integrated in the community rather than detached and isolated. Foster lines of communication between the generations. Many important aspects of life require skills and insights available only to those who have the wisdom of experience. The knowledge you have acquired over the years may now serve a greater purpose and be passed on to the young. Your curiosity is appreciated too; remain inquisitive about what younger people are doing and thinking, because they are dealing with the world your generation has built, and confronting a different set of challenges from the ones you had to deal with.

If you are reading this book as an older person, remember that there is no excuse for being out of touch. The speed of change may be such that much of what you learned socially and professionally is irrelevant, but you can adapt it to present circumstances if you know what they are – and you have no excuse to remain in ignorance. You are statistically among the most privileged people on the planet, and as such, you are able to keep track of events and technological developments from around the world instantly, in a way that has never been possible before.

To make a valuable contribution and be positively interested is constructive; to display bitterness and resentment towards the new young world is not.

Health

Today, in the industrialised world, anything seems possible. You may expect to live longer than your parents. You have access to medicine to alleviate almost all minor health complaints. Medical services can treat nearly all the serious ailments; you may if necessary receive transplanted organs. And if you wish to alter or reconstruct your appearance, there is cosmetic surgery. You can now choose how to present yourself to the world, and as you are influenced by society you may have developed an urge to compete in presenting yourself well, so that you will not be forgotten or dismissed as you grow older.

Fear of death

As you age, the possibility of your own death may become a thought lingering in the background of your every waking minute. This is simply fear; it is not rational, but the product of pervasive emotion, for you may have four or five decades, or longer, yet to live.

Fear of death can bring death closer. Allow the fear to manifest itself, and you develop weaknesses. The slightest discomfort or unease makes you feel your time has come. All you are really doing is encouraging tension, which makes you vulnerable to attack from illness.

12 Manifestations of an unquiet mind

Illness

When your emotions conflict with your mind's natural, logical pull towards self-determination, negative effects ensue. Resentment or guilt or fear start to gnaw at your thoughts. An internal battle begins and unhappiness makes you vulnerable to extremes of emotion. Your bodily energies become imbalanced; guilt may drive you to self-destructive actions as your emotional reactions spiral out of control. Sometimes this self-destruction works directly from your mind to your brain, which refuses to make connections or begins to distort the messages which normally defend your body.

All illnesses have different labels, fall into different categories and affect different parts of you. Yet they have something in common: they restrict and weaken you. You are no longer free. The creative freedom you should be using to create your own, self-determined future is directed, instead, towards your illness; your imagination starts to work against you.

When you are ill, half-forgotten suggestions and instructions resound in your mind. Reprimands and negative opinions come back and you feel small again. Once again someone who does not know you or understand you is ordering you about, telling you what you ought to do.

Whether you are the Prime Minister or a beggar, you will

be especially susceptible to hostility and hopeless negativity when you are weak. Your brain and body, which are physical, work as your mind does in this respect. During illness they become even more vulnerable.

Yet when the cycle of your mood and your health is at its lowest, you can begin to transform yourself and rise again to be stronger than ever. Your will is powerful, and refuses to repeat history; you dismiss all previous negativity and all condemnation by others. Those remarks and attitudes from long ago had their uses – they showed you, in due course, how to search within yourself for the confidence to brush them off. But you no longer need them.

Your mind can drive out pain and discomfort. The more you concentrate on it, the more energy you develop and the more empowered you become. Now you are refusing to repeat history; you are becoming truly self-determined.

Defensiveness

Go about in a state of quiet concentration on all around you, and give yourself time to absorb the suggestions and instructions transmitted by your mind. If you do not, you may miss the truth of a situation because you are blinded by emotion, and then you will be vulnerable. Instead of being open to suggestion, you will perceive everything that does not chime with your emotions as negative; you will be defensive when you are being helped.

Be receptive to suggestions for they may hold hidden messages that will become clear to you later. Resentment and rejection breed ignorance, and ignorance never finds solutions. Just one suggestion could hold the key to freedom.

Your senses are constantly alert, and they include those senses called psychic or spiritual: the 'sixth sense'. By nature you constantly scan and measure changes in the atmosphere around you. Once you feel you are fully aware of the implications of your feelings, you feel calm and prepared. You can bring awareness and motivation to the present moment and more easily reach your objectives in life. Accumulating understanding in this way triggers new ideas.

Contagious emotions

Misery loves company. You will find that sorrow and depression are capable of swift replication; they spread like a contagious disease.

Your cells split, divide, become copies of each other. You are programmed to regenerate, and your emotions to spread like the pain from a pinprick, spreading outwards from a tiny spot. And in the greater world your emotions influence those of others and the fears and insecurities prevalent in your society influence you.

The contagiousness of feelings is visible. If you see a person yawning, you will probably, involuntarily, do the same. Maybe just hearing the yawn will be enough. You will start to laugh when you see other people helpless with mirth, and be moved to tears by the weeping of a stranger. The personal connection isn't important; it is a fact that emotions are contagious.

So take care. Examine what is going on. Are these really your emotions, or have you just become infected in the spirit of the moment? Perhaps you are making yourself feel worse by accepting pity you really don't need, and allowing it to replicate itself inside you? This is easily done. When you say you're unwell, people are sorry for you. Their pity makes you feel like an invalid. You examine your body anxiously; you are worried; you identify previously ignored difficulties and discomforts and retrieve earlier aches and pains from your memory. In no time you have constructed a picture of yourself as a long-term sick person. Your mild curiosity has grown into a huge nagging anxiety. You begin to find what you were looking for, whether it is there or not.

Calm down and identify the contagious emotion that brought you to this state.

Another contagious emotion is status insecurity. The pressure is on; you are supposed to be perfect. You are invited to study images of perfection on billboards and in newspapers, and to copy them. (Of course your mind would tell you that you don't have to copy anybody, but if you don't run with the herd, you are supposed to feel inferior.) Your natural tendency is to mimic what everyone else is feeling and doing. You seek approval (forgetting that those whose approval you seek have insecurities of their own).

For instance, you may betold that if you have any excess fat, you have a problem. You are subtly taught to feel contempt towards fat people, and if you are among them, to shape up or feel bad. Overweight becomes associated with low status.

This is not the only taboo. If you are young, fit, slim and healthy, then you will almost certainly catch and mimic some other anxiety about your own appearance. Tampering with yourself for cosmetic purposes can damage your mental and physical, and financial, health.

It is time to feel satisfied with the face and body nature has given you. Accept yourself, and be proud. Being confident is the key to a healthy state of mind, one which helps your own brain and body to express the person you are.

Faking it

Suppose you seek to change something about yourself, because you are convinced that by doing so you will be happy. How far are you going to go? Are you going to start with one aspect of yourself, and carry on until you have attained perfection? Will you ever be happy to look less than perfect?

Will this cosmetic change slow your ageing process? Will it make you more confident? Or will it give you false confidence, as fake as the new nose or the new flat tummy?

If your confidence is superficial, it will endure only so long as the cosmetic change brings you approval. As you get used to living as your new self and find that much about your life doesn't change, your fears and discontents return. You start to fixate on something else as the cause of your unhappiness. And all the time, your relationships with other people are superficial; your interactions are too dependent on your appearance to have any real value.

Or will cosmetic change give you the confidence to change other things about the way you conduct your life? Unless you are willing to work with yourself as you truly are, you are destined for disappointment. Appearances affect your life to a lesser extent than you may think. Your real strengths come from within. Only when the cosmetic changes have become an insignificant part of who you are, and your confidence is strong and based on the changes you have made, will your mind be free; only then will you be free of discontent and insecurity.

Under-achievement

Did you have a good education? Some of the best-educated people would say no, for they feel that they were tied to an exam system, while their natural talents were not given time or encouragement to blossom. Inappropriate schooling can crush or deform the minds of children. Creativity should be valued as much as intellect and obedience. Everyone possesses talents, and when people are encouraged to fulfil themselves a dynamic force is released and a promising future develops for future generations.

Most schools fail to teach children to know their own mind. Without some understanding of how to handle life emotionally, mentally, physically and spiritually, all other education can go awry. Yet life skills like these are often overlooked or dismissed. Children are not taught strength of mind. They do not know how to listen to their own minds or respect them. Instead they are pushed into a mould, and are expected to seek approval from society, or their elders, or their peers, because conformity and mediocre obedience are deemed more important than thinking skills, an analytic critical mind, and creativity. The result may be unhappy adults, who waste valuable time in their search for what they really want out of life.

Depression

Depression is simply your mind alerting you from within to pay attention. You find yourself in darkness, but you must take the opportunity that this darkness offers you to communicate with your mind, for you are wonderfully sensitive at such times, and open to hearing your inner voice.

When you are depressed, your posture changes. You walk as though weighed down by care. Your shoulders curve, you stoop, your head is heavy and bowed. This is a danger sign; pay attention, stand up straight, breathe deeply, spend time and work out what is going wrong in your life.

If you pay no attention, you may never stand up straight to face the world again. We have all seen people who always look slumped and careworn. They are never really happy. Something is off track in their lives, but they have ignored the warning signs, and live out their days in endurance, not in joy.

Eliminate the obvious physical reasons why you might be depressed. Is your diet inadequate? A low or unbalanced intake of vitamins and minerals will affect your mood. So will smoking and drinking and certain other drugs including prescribed ones. If you don't drink enough water you will get headachey and fractious; if you get too little exercise you will get fat. As a result, you feel bad about yourself and don't perform as well as you should. A downward spiral into long-term depression can start with something as simple as this.

Is it a bad time of year for you? High barometric pressure

can have a physical effect on our mood and so can poor light. Pressure fluctuates quite quickly, but if you suffer from Seasonal Affective Disorder you can help yourself with easily available light therapy.

You must remember that mild depression is a perfectly natural part of the cycle of life. You may know the pattern; you start by feeling quite literally 'low'. Everything in your life seems meaningless and dull and sometimes annoying, and you are irritable and quick to take offence. You know something is not quite right, but you don't know what it is. Your thoughts and anxieties start going round in ever-decreasing circles. Your breathing is shallow and you feel deflated, like a balloon with the air disappearing. You are always tired and often sleepless; sometimes you oversleep, and then you feel more unhappy than ever.

The constant tiredness of depression is another sign that your unconscious mind requires attention, for the semi-conscious states of mind you are in when you drift off to sleep and slowly awaken are those in which you can most easily perceive the revelations your mind is offering. Also you need to mimic lifelessness and be still and focused, to detach from the present and apply your thoughts. You will lie still and allow the darkness to envelop you and yield up its secrets, so that the changes you make will be the right ones.

So befriend your depression: learn to open your mind to all you can learn from it. Out of hopelessness more energy will spring, as you start to think with resolution and method, and dream up and plan the changes you can make. Depressions are not there to destroy you. Simply accustom yourself to being alone with your thoughts, and do not let emotion drive them.

Don't feel alienated, or think that no one else can possibly imagine the depth and darkness that you are facing. It's not true. Everyone has survived many depressions, superficial or deep, because everything we do in this life goes in cycles of sleep and awakening, activity and lull.

Don't feel obsessive about the past, either; once you have

identified something unpleasant in your memory, drag it out, take a good look and decide to throw it away. Otherwise you will waste a great deal of time mentally packing and unpacking your own baggage. Dump it once and for all.

Delusions

It is possible for the balance of your mind to be disturbed, and your sense of identity fractured, to the extent that you exhibit signs of mental illness. Among the commonest of these illnesses is 'schizophrenia,' the usual medical diagnosis for a person whose perception of day-to-day life is psychotic, or seriously distorted from the norm. In this state, you may perceive (literally see or hear) events or objects, remarks or people that are imperceptible to others. Your perceptions of space and time may also deviate from anything that might be useful to you. All these things are perfectly real to you, but to everyone else they appear delusional.

Since mentally you are adrift and alone in a different world from the rest of us, you can, quite naturally, become incomprehensible – or terrified. At worst you may become angry and harm yourself or other people. Alienation, fear and anger are horrible emotions and you and those around you suffer on your behalf, so psychiatric help is usually sought.

Psychiatrists will address your emotions; and having listened, will treat your symptoms with drugs. The older anti-psychotic drugs have humiliating side-effects, and even the newer ones act by suppressing many emotions, so even these can leave you feeling inadequate. You don't want to have to take tablets for the rest of your life; you probably began to exhibit symptoms in your late teens or early twenties, and foresee decades of dependence ahead; it's mortifying. But the alternative is miserable, a life of anxiety for yourself and those around you, interspersed with occasional stays in hospital. All this can add depression to your disturbance.

But you and those around you *expect* to find a reliable cure in chemicals.

There is an alternative. Your main hurdle is going to be believing that it will work. You can learn to get in touch with your mind and tell it that it does not need help, but can maintain control without drugs. Your mind, that tiny part of yourself that is desperately trying to keep its bearings throughout your worst psychotic moments, can be made stronger and more accessible until you are fully in control.

If you are nervous of giving up the drugs that have become a crutch, then begin by recognising that your mind *can* control what happens to your body. Think of the placebo effect, where those who believe that a drug will make them better do, in fact, get better. You know this happens. It is an example in which the mind's positive ability – its ability to preserve you from harm – has been harnessed, albeit unwittingly.

Your delusions, so-called, are medically treated as a biochemical disorder, so there is no reason why the same principle should not work on them. And when you learn to instruct your mind, it will start to work for you. You must first develop, by deep breathing and insight, your mind's ability to provide positive reinforcement.

Phobias and panics

Phobias are secret, irrational fears which limit your life; the threat, which is usually non-existent, can grow to terrifying proportions in your imagination.

Perhaps you are afraid of spiders. The fact is, that unless you plan to breed them or live with them on a daily basis, say, in the Amazonian jungle, then you should not have to care whether you fear spiders or not. If you were stuck in a room with a spider, your self-preserving attack instinct would override the panicky phobic response and allow you to destroy the spider in an impeccable manner to ensure your own personal safety. The same principle applies to heights. If you do not need to climb onto high ledges there is no need to worry about them. You can be certain that if you had to climb a great height in order to save your life, you would do so; the instinct for self-preservation would override your panic.

Panic attacks can be caused by anxiety, as well as by phobias. Everything seems to be racing by, you can hardly breathe and your heart rate increases. You are preternaturally alert, fearful of the unknown. Your fearful imaginings fuel your panic. If this happens in a nightmare, you awake in dread; when it happens in your waking hours, you are in a state of emotional collapse.

Don't panic. Take a deep breath and think. Better still, give way to your real feelings at last – whether it's your impulse to kill a spider, to abseil down a building, or to burst into tears. You cannot hide from life. Look at your panic attacks objectively and ask yourself whether you are panicking because of a genuine threat or a perceived one. Ask your mind: why did you create this phobia and how are you going to deal with it? Is it wrecking your life or can you happily live with it? What anxiety is making you panic? Your emotions may lead you to deny certain uncomfortable truths; your mind will not.

Morbid imaginings

All over the world people use different sorts of paraphernalia to 'communicate with the dead'. These range from voodoo rituals to the Ouija board, which many people see as a game. In the hands of vulnerable people, it is not a game. When a group of people call up 'the spirits of the departed' and don't not know how to deal with the consequences, some among their number may become needlessly distressed. Whether this is mass hysteria or whether you believe in it makes no difference; people who are already fragile can be driven to terror. The fear they feel is almost impossible to deal with alone, and may tip them permanently into mental illness. Much better that you should never get involved in this kind of so-called spirit communication. Accept what you are given by the spirit that is within you, and don't meddle with charlatans. You need to be aware of your own superstitions and dreads, which may go deeper than you think, and children in particular should not be allowed anywhere near Ouija boards or séances.

If you have lost someone dear to you, let them go. Don't pervert their memory with your own emotions. Accept their passing. Release them, and nourish your thoughts with the memories they left behind and the good they did.

Extreme volatility

When you are disordered, that is to say when the balance of your mind is slightly disturbed, your mood swings violently between negative and positive.

At such times, achieving the correct balance is particularly difficult. You feel so insignificant as a person that you seem to fade; you don't have much effect on the world and you know it, and people sense this and take you at your own valuation. We are all aware of our own imperfections, but if you get them out of proportion you can think yourself into a negative state of mind which becomes a self-fulfilling prophecy. You either escape into self-destructive behaviour, or hide away from the world.

On the other hand, you may veer dramatically towards the opposite pole and become exaggeratedly positive about yourself.

You develop a false claim to superiority; your ego overwhelms your mind with selfishness, boastfulness, and the typical behaviour of a small frightened trapped being – you are like The Mouse that Roared. Such a state of mind destroys other people, as you make your power manifest. You try to make your fantasies come true; the world must bend to your emotion-driven will. The behaviour you exhibit depletes your own emotional energy in such a way that if ultimately you are forced to comply with the will of others, you respond with frustration and anger. Your emotions overwhelm your mind and there is no balance.

At times like these, you must balance positive and negative. Approach your innermost desires with respect, and recognise that you should use them to serve your progress and development, not to destroy yourself or other people. Your ultimate objective has to be achieved by the power of your mind. Your own unique equipoise will attract like-minded people and help to keep you on the right path.

Being impressionable

Whatever may be your direction in life, make sure that you first remain in touch with yourself. Protect *yourself*. This means more than protecting your material interests; it means protecting your thoughts and ideas from negativity and harm. Carelessness in this regard is damaging. It will lead to anxiety and in the extreme, depression. The balance of your mind may become unstable, and you will start to think there is some inadequacy in yourself that makes you stuck, powerless and unable to act.

You have a dream, you have an imagination and you have fantasies. When you are engaged in creative work you may become entirely oblivious to what is around you; you are in your element and feel healthy and strong as you begin to make things happen. But it is when your passion becomes *obsession* that you are in danger. When your fantasies constantly repeat themselves you become obsessive. In this frame of mind impressions are allowed to cause deep mental wounds, and you risk sacrificing your present, as well as your future health. Obsessiveness is an obvious failure, and failure often triggers self-punishment.

At this point, remember all you know about the need to make sacrifices. In the natural pattern of existence, the old is sacrificed to make room for the new. If you do not allow your old breath to escape and disappear, you cannot take in a new one. You must exhale to be able to inhale. In all that you do, you have to sacrifice one thing for another. Sacrifice is a natural pattern of existence, for you always have to sacrifice something of the past to create a better future and in order to create and build, you sacrifice time.

13 Blessings and sacrifices

Acceptance: marriage

When you approve of a situation or a proposal, you give it your blessing; when you receive the blessing of someone you respect, you feel at peace. Sometimes this may have a lot to do with a sense of belonging – a sense of being accepted.

If you decide to get married, you can look forward to receiving the blessing of the wider community or of the elders of your church. They witness and accept that you and your partner are making binding promises to each other. However, many people fail to keep those promises, and if you are among them, you will know that the blessing turns bitter; the memory of it is now a guilty reminder that you carry forward for the rest of your days.

As you develop, even after your marriage, your needs and desires develop too. They may remain unfulfilled, causing you discontent. An unsullied blessing allied with total fulfilment naturally exists, but many people do not find these things. Then they have to choose whether to retain the approval of others, or to listen to their own minds.

Making an agreement such as marriage is a way of bonding, but the wedding ceremony may become an end in itself. Because of the wedding, new emotions intervene. It is a new beginning and an official milestone in both your lives, so you are more assertive than usual. You are setting the seal on something: from now on, this is how things will be.

Can it work? Change is inevitable. For how long can you both stay the same? It is impossible to hold a thought for more than a breath. Cycles of thought are completed with every breath you take, and each breath that you take triggers a billion solutions in your mind, brain and body.

Marriage vows can give you a false sense of security. You guarantee to yourself as well as the other person that your feelings will never change. This is a promise based on emotion and made in innocence. Your mind tells you that it may be over-optimistic, since your life together could be long and eventful and no-one can foretell what effect change and growth will have. And it is your emotions that may one day lead you to some deviation from your promise.

Marriage vows can make you fearful and doubtful and guilty, for you are meant to keep promises.

If you see your marriage as essentially a contract made for legal reasons, why should there be no possibility of altering the contract by mutual consent? The law created these vows and the law itself can overturn them. Are your marriage vows to bind you forever in any circumstances?

What is, or was, the reason for your marriage? Most people who marry do so because they feel drawn to each other by a kind of magnetism. The other person occupies the whole of their emotions.

If the reason is magnetic sexual attraction, you can be certain that one party, at some point, will be drawn just as strongly to other aspects of life and the sexual aspect will die away. The union then becomes satisfactory for one and not for the other.

If the attraction is purely physical, your union will have an even shorter lifespan. This is because if you are attracted solely by the way someone looks, you can easily be attracted to someone else.

Most people's desires, emotions and imaginative

expectations of their marriage partner exceed anything they can realistically expect to find. It is the unexpected unions that have the best possible chance of working long term because they are based on a complex nexus of attraction and conflict. If you are fortunate enough to find a partner like this, you will get used to making concessions and allowances, to learning new things and remaining interested in each other. Your mind opens when you learn to adapt and adopt in this way, for there is a power that feels almost spiritual, which makes you ignore any physical deterioration. A kind of unity evolves and develops between your two minds, inspiring mutual emotions and creating ongoing interest.

Separation of husband and wife, however, is immensely traumatising. If you suffer this it may overwhelm you, especially if a third party is involved. No authority will halt or overturn the guilt you feel, and it will deprive both of you of precious time and space in life. The sense of loss is immeasurable.

Yet you know that with the end of a cycle, a new one begins. If you are to gain by change, you can expect to make sacrifices. This is a fact demonstrated every day of your life. So although some people may prefer to stay grieving, discontented and unfulfilled, others will decide they cannot and should not. It is a matter of choice. No-one can judge who is right.

Birth

Either or both parents of a baby may become depressed because the start of one life is in some senses the end of another. Things change, and never more so than with the first child. If, as a new parent, you feel over-awed at the responsibility you have taken on, then this is perfectly natural – just as it is natural to feel that you have lost something by becoming a parent. You have. Life will never be the quite the same again, but it's more than that. You are no longer the future; interest has passed to the next generation. You are no longer, in fact, the most important person in the room, or in your world – from now on, this small person has the advantage of you.

The dynamics of a family change when a new baby arrives. In the worst cases the husband feels alienated and ignored, the other children are jealous, the baby has infant eczema, and hormonal changes have given the new mother more than the usual few days of baby blues; she has post-natal depression and is weeping all the time. Nobody can make time to deal with their feelings because the adults are frantically busy and the children are trying to find distraction from the chaos.

This is time to act in a counter-intuitive way. *Stop*. Examine your emotions. How do you feel? What are you afraid of? What is the worst that can happen here? What does the baby want? Have you been driving yourself too hard?

What everybody wants is time. Let your mind control your emotions. Pay attention to the emotions of everyone else. Show them you respect how they feel. How are things going to be in six months' time? Can you get through this together? Think about it; you will find that with a relaxed attitude to unimportant matters, and more time spent thinking and talking, you can.

Endings and transitions

Any major change – the ending of a marriage, a career, the loss of some physical capacity or a bereavement – changes everything in your life and everything in your mind and your emotions. You have to set your previous life aside and absorb a new atmosphere. You have to accept harsh reality, but also to accept that from change some benefits are possible. However terrible the upheaval may seem, you must look upon the experience as a blessing which will bring new opportunities.

So be ready to accept what happens. For any change, even the ending of a life, mus be understood and acknowledged so that its energy can be released. All you may have is a memory, but it is a memory full of knowledge and wisdom which will in due course contribute to your own life.

The ending may take you to the deepest place in your mind, a depression that leaves you disassociated from your physical existence. Do not dwell in the darkness. Stay aware and alert and prepared to accept. Understand that your life has cycles every one of which has a beginning and an end. You cannot repeat a cycle, just as you can never precisely repeat the emotions you experienced in the past. If you make the mistake of trying to live in the past, you can easily remain in the dark and waste a precious lifetime.

Endings are part of our existence. When you learn to exercise the power of your mind, you will understand that these transitions in your life will guide you towards your destiny, a destiny so vital and relevant that it seems predestined rather than conceived by yourself. Understand that beyond darkness there is light.

Your mind functions at its highest level at times of transition. You have to act, you have to think, and your emotions are fully engaged. Your mind, body, brain and heart operate at full capacity to achieve your goals.

Sacrifice

If you sincerely seek a change in your life, don't allow emotion alone to drive you. Instead apply your mind's power to creating small changes that together form the whole. You have to make sacrifices in order to achieve change; yet complications may arise if you decide you must suppress aspects of your personality, thoughts and imagination in order to change. If you find it difficult, despite your best intentions, to adapt, adjust and adopt new people and places, ideas and approaches to life, then change is going to be impossible.

A person who passionately desires another may sacrifice something of himself or herself in order to become the 'other' that the beloved wants and approves of. A blessing and a promise are made to work towards fulfilment of the most powerful inner drives; and this is natural. However, it is temporary.

If you are employed, you may sacrifice something of yourself in order to please your employer. All you do must comply with the rules. You and your colleagues jostle for approval, acceptance and promotion. You feel unable to express an independent thought or speak your mind. Your stifled creativity finds release in office politics. Your discontent becomes evident and there is a pervasive unease. As this goes on, your focus on promotion may make you forget what you are trying to achieve for yourself through your work.

In families, brothers and sisters and even parents and grandparents compete for respect and admiration and praise from all the others. You all want to be loved, but you all want to be loved most of all for your special talents. This is so difficult that children may stifle their curiosity and adults assume greater wisdom than they have, in a desire to find approval. By sacrificing something of themselves, they gain peace at the expense of self-respect.

Among friends, a natural leader often emerges. This is usually someone who enjoys a sense of freedom that the others lack. This person is therefore seen as the most knowledgeable and experienced: the one to copy in order to gain approval. Yet imitation is impossible, since the key to that person's personality is that he or she doesn't copy anyone else, and doesn't sacrifice anything of herself, but knows her own mind and behaves accordingly.

With strangers, you naturally put your defences up. The presence of strangers makes most of us uneasy; we are feeling our way. Yet if you keep quiet, refusing to show your hand, the implication is that you are taking the measure of the stranger in order not to offend them. The sacrifice here is your self-protectiveness; if you are convinced that your motives are pure, you have nothing to fear by revealing your own mind.

The threat of disapproval

In organised religions, costumes and rituals and ceremonial are a way of demonstrating superiority and authority, and other organisations use similar status indicators. Perhaps you do not think of the clothes you wear and the things you do as indicators of high status but they often are; maybe this is the way we seek acknowledgement of our presence.

If you pray, you do not do so in expectation of offending your god. On the contrary, you do so while seeking the approval of a god or a prophet. Prayers are usually directed towards something out there, unseen with the conscious eye, but felt in spirit. The stronger the prayer the further it reaches. When your emotions are in turmoil you seek solace from your god. You direct your prayers to the source of your belief. When you are in the deepest difficulty, your prayer asks your god to be merciful.

Your fear that you have done wrong may make you feel guilty in the sight of your god, and your religion may impose prayer as a duty. You are supposed to be cleansed from wrongdoing by prayer. Your god approves your prayer and you no longer feel guilty.

In no time at all, you become reliant on this kind of arrangement. Your dependency upon this exchange of wrongdoing for prayer makes you feel safe. You can carry on behaving as you did before, as long as you pray for forgiveness from time to time. You are seeking approval from the unknown, and invisible, and you can easily convince yourself that forgiveness is granted; if you do not, your priest will.

This cycle guarantees that you will repeat the same mistakes again and again, rather than learning independence and true self-respect and self-confidence. It renders reason redundant, and change too. There is no incentive to seek the answers in your own mind and every incentive to act according to selfish emotion, ask forgiveness and feel safe.

These traditions provide the psychological structure for

unthinking self-satisfaction. You can lead your entire life this way, through a series of routine actions and reactions, implemented in every area of your life.

Rejection

When approval is withheld, rejection may leave scars that last a long time and affect you in many ways. You feel limited by it, and constricted to achieve less. You become unhappy. You may become prejudiced and careless of the feelings of others; you may feel alienated by others, because you feel you no longer belong. Inside, you are lost. Secretly you crave blessing and approval and inclusion in the group.

This can make you totally submissive. You accept your fate without conflict because it is more comfortable to do so. You are so afraid of being excluded that you change nothing, do nothing, say nothing, make no mark. At least this way nobody has anything to criticise. And the strategy, such as it is, allows you to feel superficially secure.

Yet at a deep level all you crave is approval for every small choice you make. You cannot feel secure until you have support and encouragement; you do not have the courage of your own convictions, but constantly look to others for confirmation that what you are doing is correct. Only then can you feel that you belong.

We must respect each other without interference and give that respect unconditionally; we should expect to be respected back.

14 Unconscious talents

Detachment

As soon as you walk out of your front door you encounter feelings, reactions, thought and energy in various forms. You are bombarded by impressions: of colour, noise, changes in temperature. All your senses are active. Your sensory reactions provoke journeys in your memory and imagination. You start to think of the people you may enounter, and when people pass you in the street you scan, without thinking, the energy they project: are they happy, sad or angry? You get an impression of their lifestyle, or they may bring to mind someone you know – vividly, with dialogue and voices and visions of moments in their lives when you were present.

All this happens at a level of consciousness of which you are barely aware, as you concentrate on transient stimuli.

If you observe your own reactions to the hubbub of daily life, and try to analyse them, you will start to recognise the underlying emotional responses you are having and use them to your advantage. But if you reject these stimuli, you will be overcome by exhaustion, because they are so many and varied. Should the dramatic reactions provoked by all that you see and hear every day be allowed to overpower you, they will limit you; you'll refuse to take in one more impression. The resulting constraint will affect your physical being.

So stay in control; you will perceive the rich variety of life as vividly as ever, but will not be overwhelmed, for you will have instructed your mind to reduce the impact to manageable proportions.

Whenever you find yourself over-stimulated by external things, make a deliberate effort to remain connected with your mind. You will find that the whole experience changes. You will become expert at communicating with your inner mind, and your intuitive understanding of people and situations will increase dramatically.

Telepathy and psychic ability

There is nothing mystic about telepathy or psychic ability. They are among many unconscious talents you have that you don't know you use. Yet they are essential tools for your survival, since telepathic and psychic communications arise from such a deep level that they are *true*; this being so, they bring deeper awareness and save precious life time.

Everyone should strive to develop these rewarding natural attributes and everyone can. All you have to do is *become one with your mind.* You will only achieve this by practice: by spending time learning to become one with your mind, demanding and commanding from your mind that it connect with your consciousness.

All existence relies on communication, and the starting point of human communication is the brain. All over your body there are physical nerve cells that transmit messages to your brain. Your brain receives a constant stream of information from them: they transmit, below your consciousness, your ever-present awareness of changes in temperature and humidity, noise levels and hidden danger. This unseen, unheard perpetual response of the brain to sensitive stimuli is described as intuition, or more impressively psychic ability, and (when it reaches a higher order altogether) as a talent for telepathy.

Perhaps you have had the experience, which is common, of talking or thinking about someone you know just seconds before they suddenly appear or phone you. This always comes as a shock, yet it can be explained. Your mind understands, as the other person does, that it's about time you made contact; your mind therefore prepares you for the encounter. Something similar happens in many other situations: a flash of insight which is often a warning, sometimes a wish, but which tells you what is about to happen *because at the level of the mind, you already know.*

Telepathy works in the same way, except there are emotional connections and interactions with other people. When you are talking to somebody, maybe you say the same thing at once, or almost do – and it's a meeting of minds; you are matching one another's intuition.

Concentrate on your mind's perception of what the other is thinking, match it, and you will find that you can influence the thoughts of others in the way that people call telepathy. If you purify and focus your own thoughts, you will become sensitive to the emotionally charged projections of thought from others. You may not be aware of it, but at a deep level you will be reading eye movement and interpreting body language and the fleeting, barely visible movements of thousands of facial muscles.

Mediums imagine that they can communicate with the dead; they are either reading signals from the living, or are unusually sensitive to the minute physical changes in temperature and light which make them imagine that apparitions are present.

Developing your intuitive faculties

If you work hard to improve your 'telepathic' and 'psychic' talents you will experience life more fully; your whole being will focus powerfully at moments of threat or joy.

Once you have dared to relinquish control and permit your mind to take over, you learn to open up more and more. Your mind can create the circumstances and reactions which are required for you to reach your destiny; simply pay attention when it suggests ways to improve and evolve.

You will need to spend some time alone with your mind, breathing deeply to increase the oxygen supply to your brain which will help you to concentrate. Instruct your mind to *tell you what you know you know.* Let your mind know you can be trusted to listen. You can be trusted to use your mind for your own good and the good of mankind.

Pay attention to the silence.

Voices may come, or you may visualise solutions. You will almost certainly find it helpful to release your power of automatic writing. Anyone can do it, and if you are patient and determined your mind will open to an outpouring of energy you never knew you had. Your personality will become vivid to you, your sense of self will be stronger than ever before, and all your actions will feel inspired.

Exercise your talents for greater insight; exercise, test and test again. Be determined, for your mind will always be open to you when you are desperate for solutions. It will not deal with mundane emotional issues, but at these important times it will use the logic of nature itself in a dispassionate way. Acknowledge the responses of your mind by silently answering Yes or No, and allow everything else to manifest itself according to your desires and your aims.

You may literally hear a voice when you are about to make a decision; the voice is your intuition – your mind's instruction. You may do as it says, or disregard it and do what you want. If you ignore the advice, though, you usually regret it later.

Sometimes situations change suddently without warning. If you are not in regular contact with your mind, the sudden upheaval will render you deaf to its advice; but if you are in the habit of communicating with your mind, you will be ready to trust your intuition. When you ask your mind to respond, all you will get is a plain Yes or No. From then on, it's up to you to use your wisdom and determination to carry out your plan.

Seclusion

Exploring your own mind can be a long-drawn-out process. If you are to find answers deep within, you will have to isolate yourself from the world. You will be calm; your mind will not reveal all its secrets at once, but will silently help you to understand and grow.

Imagine being a recluse: a quiet isolated person, analysing, calculating, weighing, searching, and questioning in silence for solutions or mind-expanding insights. You would have to exercise prudence. You would have to listen and assess possibilities before carrying them to their logical conclusions.

You can follow this course without entirely retiring from your daily life. Simply accept that you must think like a seer or a wise recluse; you must look before you leap, checking for interference from emotions that will lead you astray. If, in such a state, you detach from emotion you can analyse with a clear head.

But if you can truly retreat from the world for even a short time, you will not regret it. You will deliberately ignore everyday thoughts and insist on being at one with your mind. Allow nothing else to intrude. Remember that you are the product of a unity of positive and negative; your breath brings to life all that you seek.

A temporary withdrawal from life's struggle is of inestimable value, for the sake of something as deeply spiritual as the exploration of your mind. If you ask your god for a change, nothing happens. Yet when you ask your own mind, energies begin to shift and things begin to move and transform. They will continue to do so on every level of your existence, not just in material things.

There can be no progress without thought or planning and

true wisdom comes from within. As you slow your thoughts down, meanings which were hidden before suddenly become clear. Isolated within your own mind, you will be in command, able to control the rate of your progress, ready to use the energy generated by recent change. or to overcome obstacles; to confront events in their darkness, or to emerge out of the darkness into light.

Your mind holds a memory of the confidence to make anything possible. Once you are in touch with it, your attitude will bring leadership and success, as you confront the world spiritually free from inhibitions, limitations and restrictions.

Charlatans and showmen, wizards and experts

Exercise your mind in silence. Do not tell the world of your newly discovered talents, or try to tell other people's fortunes. Keep your gift to yourself, for at some point easy communication with your mind will help you immensely in your journey through life.

Don't tarnish your gifts with claims of magical or mysterious powers, nor allow yourself to be influenced by those who feel you should engage with your mind in the course of a ritual or ceremony. No secret codes or magic words will widen, speed up, or slow down the process. We all possess the ability to engage in a dialogue with the mind and we all develop individually. Unfortunately, most of us are too distracted by life; our gift remains unopened and forgotten.

People who claim to engage with the mind can easily convince others that they are superior, but they are not. Your mind is simply hidden and mysterious, but it is accessible, so do not fall victim to mediums, psychoanalysts, alternative therapists or medical practitioners who exercise their apparent superiority with great ignorance.

Conventional medical diagnoses are usually based on universal physical principles without regard to the patient's mental and emotional state, where a holistic diagnosis would take into account all the variations which may affect illness. A tic or some visible tension is easy enough to see, but to find out which of many possible reasons lies behind it is more difficult; emotional reactions are not universal and a hurried misdiagnosis can damage a vulnerable individual.

Hypnotists divert consciousness while they programme the subconscious mind to direct the consciousness towards certain modes of behaviour. This programming lasts only if you are a desperate seeker. Most hypnotic instruction is short-lived, and when it fades traumatic memories may remain unresolved.

Stage hypnotists may overpower the consciousness of their subjects so far as to put them to sleep; they then treat the subject with disdain, as the audience enjoys identifying with the apparent superiority of the hypnotist. If you are not fully awake and alert, allow no-one else to have direct communication with your mind for the results may not change your behaviour in a productive way.

You can quite usefully hypnotise yourself. Simply get in touch with your mind and instruct it as a hypnotist would. Focus on your mind, repeat your instruction, and you will soon begin to notice the positive changes in your behaviour that you wanted. This kind of self-hypnosis strengthens you and enables you to surmount obstacles in your path.

You will come across people who claim to be 'mind control experts'; some are stage performers, while others are researchers who simply attack the whole idea. The question you need to ask is: if a person could really control the mind of another, why would they use this extraordinary gift to play tricks on other people and belittle them in the eyes of others? As for those researchers who claim to be experts, they tend to have come recently to the field and have a lot to learn.

15 Religious faith

Political authority

If you subscribe to one of the major religious faiths, you will be familiar with the idea that your god is omnipotent, without boundaries. It follows that this omnipotent being requires no human intervention between itself and your mind. You also believe that this being is essentially benevolent towards you, and wishes you well; therefore fear is redundant.

You have, therefore, no cause to support any of the great religions. Laudable as their efforts may be in many respects, they have historically been divisive. From earliest times, religion has been used to reinforce political power. Claims to superior understanding of matters mystical, spiritual and paranormal were claims to political leadership. Mysticism became a weapon, a way of making people scared of the powers of a priestly class. Natural democracy was replaced by religious dictatorship in theocratic regimes that ruled, like any other, by a combination of fear and favour, with the added threat of reward or punishment in the afterlife.

Even today, fear of the unknown continues to underpin much religious teaching. Most religions thrive on censorship and rely on it, too; they do not countenance questioning. Those born into the religious community are considered heretical if they question and blasphemous if they choose to ridicule religious beliefs.

Identity

All the major world religions co-opt their members from the children of believers. A branding ceremony such as christening or circumcision takes place before children are old enough to make their own choice, and enjoyable family rituals around food and festivals reinforce religious identity as the individual grows up. By the time children of religious households reach adulthood, they are so accustomed to life within the religious identity that most find it comfortable, and are disinclined to question religious authority.

Yet the moment you're placed in a category, you are no longer yourself. Would your god, if you have one, want you to lose your individuality as a human being?

Conflict and division

When you are placed in a category, even a religious one, you feel like a member of a team. This is all very well but it means you consider yourselves the winning side; whether or not the world agrees with you, your god does, and your god says you are *right*.

Only this isn't a game; it is deadly serious, because you are taught to consider yourself, and your co-religionists, to be the only ones in possession of the truth – the moral authority to make judgements about right and wrong. As the strength of your moral authority will slacken unless it is enforced, those who disagree are cast out or punished as an example to others.

In consequence of this divisive tendency, all the great world religions have split into different churches and sects. In Christianity, for instance, the Catholics have an aversion to the Protestants and the Protestants mistrust the Greek Orthodox and so on. In many countries ecumenism is a minority enthusiasm and divisions thrive. Every sect and religious movement has one core belief: *we are right.*

Lies

Priests make claims about their prophets and messiahs and saints and miracles, and about the afterlife. Many of their claims are hard to believe, and those about an afterlife are a confection. Are you willing to live your life according to a set of beliefs that your rational self tells you may be nonsense?

Or are you frightened to relinquish these beliefs because you have always been told that something terrible will happen if you do? It won't.

The stories were made up to manipulate and entertain people who were simpler than you are. In the main, they did no harm and very often they were no doubt comforting. But grown-ups do not need comforting: they need control of their own minds, and a framework in which they can question what they are told without fear of recrimination.

Take, for instance, the story of Cain and Abel. They were the only children of Adam and Eve. They are supposed to have been born out of a sinful union in which their mother corrupted their father, the parents having been alone in the world at the time, except for the serpent.

Once they grew up, Cain and Abel allegedly fathered children of their own. The story does not explain how, and the reader is left to assume that they did so by incest (it must have been Eve, up to her old tricks). Or then again: two billion Christians are supposed to believe in the virgin birth, but parthogenesis is a physical impossibility in humans, so far as we know.

People feel constrained to believe these fundamentally problematic stories because they are told that questioning is a sin in itself.

Celibacy

At some time you have experienced desire. You were conceived out of an orgasm; this is nature's way. During orgasm you are overwhelmed by a feeling that is powerful, spiritual, generous and closer to godliness than any other. You were healed by it, in mind and body. So any omnipotent god would be inconsistent, to say the least, to expect its priests to abstain from the sexual act, the most important in human existence.

Yet the leader of at least one major world religion insists that this aspect of human behaviour is somehow impure: too impure for anyone to experience it without the sanction of religion, and certainly too impure for priests to indulge in, ever.

How could a just god demand celibacy? Sexual awareness and experience is fundamental to our humanity; through it we create life, and through it we come to understand love and affection on all levels.

The major monotheistic religions, while they do not all demand celibacy of their priests, nonetheless find desire sinful in some of its aspects. Their god certainly has a dark sense of humour, if human beings must suffer the torments of hell because they have experienced desire.

All this would be ludicrous, were it not for the deep and lasting pain it causes. People are made to feel guilty for sexual thoughts and actions and impulses which are completely natural. And the results can be even worse. Guilt is imposed, and abstinence enforced, so harshly that normal feelings are buried deep in the psyche, later to emerge in perverse form as sexual aggression or abuse. These tragic results are now frequently disclosed, yet those religious authorities who see sexual desire as a sin remain as adamant in defence of their faith as they ever did.

Excuses

That Christian church that expounds sexual abstinence as the highest of virtues also preaches the possibility of forgiveness. The system works like this: you ask the priest's forgiveness for a sin, and the priest, as the god's representative on earth, is supposed to believe that you are truly sorry, and will believe it as long as you perform a penance of some kind.

This is puzzling. The penance is not generally difficult, and if you are always forgiven, there is not much incentive to change your behaviour. In a way it makes sense, since so many of the sins you are supposed to have committed are perfectly harmless: lustful thoughts, perhaps, or coveting your neighbour's nice car. The god you are supposed to be worshipping made you like this, yet apparently didn't make you perfect enough for the priests.

The vengeful god

Christianity and Islam, the two largest monotheistic religions of the world, claim between them followers among about 50% of the world's six billion people, so there is a 50% chance that you are among them. If so you will be familiar with the dark and pitiless nature of the god you are required to worship and the strong reward-and-punishment element of the education inflicted upon followers' children. These emotional intrusions into sensitive young minds have a deep and lasting, illogical and unnatural effect.

Yet there are alternative beliefs; there are thinkers of genius, philosophical truth-seekers and thoughtful scientists who have contributed far more towards our evolution as human beings. In the most illiberal theocratic societies these thinkers have no voice.

Religion as a justification for aggression

In its epidemic proportions religion is destructive. Mistaken attitudes, beliefs and perceptions ripple across the face of Earth. Energies clash and create hatred and rejection, not only between societies but within families. Ignorance of the ways of others may make you fear them, and fear of the unknown can provoke you to fight.

Pause and consider this. All animals, when scared, will attack or run; we are no different. But you can, if you wish, control your impulses in a way no other animal can. If people think differently from you, you are surely intelligent enough to find out more about them, to find out what they want, to negotiate, to try to understand and to reason. If you allow religious dogma to justify a simple, brutal attack, you undermine your dignity as a human being.

As you grew up, if you were treated well by people who meant you no harm, you learned to love and respect your fellow human beings without prejudice. By nature you are probably content to let other people believe what they wish and live as they wish. You are unlikely to have been born belligerent. Since ill-will is a waste of energy it makes no sense that your god, if you have one, would wish you to bother with it for so much as one second.

Ill thoughts and needless aggression should play no part in your life. If doors open to you, walk through them; if a door remains shut, do not force it.

Death

Many religions use the fear of death as a weapon of punishment or reward. Yet when you develop a deep awareness of your mind, you protect yourself from the un-thoughtful, the innocent or the ignorant. Your mind is all that you are. Deep within your mind, your spirit drives and motivates, inspires and guides you along your path. Your spirit is part of the universe and at one with the universe. It is not an omnipotent being who seeks to judge you.

Your god is in yourself, and your mind possesses all the understanding that is necessary for your life on earth. The knowledge within your mind is as true as your first instincts, like the instinct that led you to cry for food when you were a baby. Your mind knows that you will one day die, and you have no need to fear the inevitable.

When one day you open your arms to accept death then you will do so in peace and understanding, free of fear. Why should you have anything to fear? You have been true to yourself, you have taken your place in the universe and have lived in understanding of your own mind, taking responsibility for your own actions and learning from them.

16 Spiritual empowerment

Angels

You instinctively believe that life has order and purpose and you are part of a bigger picture; and unless you are suffering from a life-threatening condition, you also have hope. If you are to act in your own best interests, you *must* have hope, that is, faith in your own future.

Whether you have faith in yourself or in a god, at your worst, most frightening times you give thanks that some external force has operated in your favour: you are still alive. These forces are sometimes called angels.

Children naturally find comfort in angels. In their innocence, they know that they require protection and if they cannot find it in the real world, they are happy to call angels into being. As adults, we know that angels are imaginary but they are as good a way as any of describing the positive forces which surround us, and events and people that cross our path bringing better times.

Of course you may deny the existence of angels, but you know that they are a way of expressing an inner search, which is real enough. You may be sceptical, but you will still silently wish for help at moments of despair.

Balance through meditation

If you are to draw on your deepest resources at will, you must achieve mental balance through meditation. Most techniques that enable you to balance positive and negative energies originated in the East, and some have become religions, with sects and disagreements and claims to superhuman abilities that may not appear particularly relevant to you. But the basic techniques, so useful to communicating with your mind, have spread widely so that wherever you live, you will find ways to learn and practice meditation.

Meditation should mean focussing on your own mind. Through meditation you will achieve emotional balance. This will affect you in every area of your life. It is certainly important enough to learn in isolation, but you do not have to go to extremes if you do not choose to. You may simply choose to begin your journey in darkness and silence, setting yourself as free as possible from the thoughts and sensations of everyday life.

As with anything else, you must be motivated if you are to apply the potential of your mind effectively. You need above all to understand yourself, for it is in your mind that the source of control lies. Once your mind is in balance, you can overcome all obstacles. With practice, you will be able to switch to a higher state at will.

An exercise

Imagine you are the only person left on earth. You start a journey in which you encounter everything nature has to offer. Everything you come across has a secret; everything works from the centre outwards. You come to hills, and don't know what lies beyond. You come to woods, and expect the unexpected. Difficulty, doubt and ignorance assail you along your journey, but you feel the earth safe beneath your feet, your imagination is fired by the colours you see, and the hills bring you closer to the stars.

Just as trees and plants grow out of the earth, human beings absorb immense energy from the world around them. Imagine walking barefoot and feel the stability and energy of the soil. Luxuriate in the sunlight, feel it on your skin, breathe in the warm air and feel the power of life it generates. You feel more energetic, more optimistic, more positive. You see and smell plants of every variety and colour and fragrance, nourished by tiny roots. You gaze down upon valleys and watch rivers flow sparkling into blue seas. As darkness approaches you see the pale moon, and feel your emotions. The moon's image remains in your thoughts as you breathe in cool air, drawing energy from the night sky. Moonlight and starlight illuminate the darkness.

You are part of the earth's energy and draw energy from the earth. Like a mother, it holds you close, and gives you life.

Inspiration

It is natural to conduct your journey through life with caution. Nature gives you fear as protection, for although it gives you life, it also has the balancing power of being able to destroy you without mercy. So while your mind's intuition may issue warnings that your conscious thoughts deny, it will also offer inspiration – solutions that allow you to overcome the obstacles ahead.

You have probably noticed that emotions concealed in your daily life often surface in the dark of night. This is not necessarily because you are suppressing them; you are busy accumulating experience and all your senses and responses must be so active that your emotional reactions may be delayed. It is not until you are alone that your mind tries to bring order out of the chaos of daily experience. In the course of the night, your positive emotions are put to use, and your mind begins to create new ways forward.

Ideas are born. You provide safety and material shelter for yourself on solid foundations; you negotiate with others and reach mutually satisfactory outcomes; you spend months or years in the effort of creating something new, and are content. Yet nature can always throw some unexpected element into your arrangements, once again challenging you to react and improve.

Success and the danger of false pride

Spiritual nourishment is the most important reward of your creative effort. It generates more power and motivates you to go further. You develop faith in what you are doing, and find that the more effort and creativity you apply to your ideas, the more fruitful they become. You delight in the world as it rewards your efforts. You display enterprise, and put to good use all that you have learned in your life. You begin to experience material well-being, and to appreciate luxury where once mere food and shelter seemed all you could possibly want. You begin to accumulate material things, and appearances matter more.

Finally you feel you have won a victory over adversity, your struggle is over, and you feel utterly elated. Can you become excessively elated by success? You can, for if you triumph in everything you do, you are unprepared for failure. Your emotional drive to achieve exactly what you want becomes so passionate that it enforces compliance; it cannot accept obstacles of any kind. False pride lies in wait with every new success.

So you need to be careful that you don't lose your sense of balance and proportion. If, in the natural order of things, your plans will bring harm, then do not pursue them. They are destined to fail, and you must know when to retire gracefully from battle. For if you begin something, and against your better judgement persist, you may find that many lives, not just your own, are badly affected.

Instead, continue to apply your mind to every problem. Now that you are in a position to overcome obstacles, you can afford high motives, and you will exercise tolerance, justice and wisdom. Yet you are still not safe from false pride, for your aims and ideals may soar so high that you are isolated. Partnerships, unions and friendships melt away because you no longer have anything in common with the people you once knew.

You have to make big decisions; you have no-one to turn to, and now you think your concerns are so important that you have no time to consult your mind. Overwhelmed by the anxieties of great responsibility, you may suffer physically and develop sadness and difficulties.

You may have great riches and feel the world is within your grasp. But take care, for if you have left humility behind on the way, you will have acquired much and gained little.

Compromise

Patience and endurance are the key to riches – spiritual and emotional riches as well as material. You cannot, unless you are willing to commit the most serious of criminal acts, physically enforce your will; you must negotiate, and this takes time.

You need to find partnerships that are balanced. Look to the interests of the other party. Matching interests will bring you together, and both parties will be willing to make some sacrifices in order to achieve an outcome that suits everyone.

If your interests are opposed from the start, then at least one side, and probably both, will always feel it is giving more than it is getting in return. Each party will start off with suspicions: one of you will feel you are being overcharged, and the other will feel underpaid; one will feel under-appreciated, and the other will feel taken for granted; one will feel bullied, and the other ignored. Whether you are individuals or governments or businesses, you may learn to live in uneasy peace but you will always resent one another.

All effective partnerships, especially those that start out perfectly balanced, undergo changes in equilibrium. Each side changes. Your needs and objectives change, and so do your perceptions of yourself and your partner. You may feel frustrated by a lack of progress, and blame the other person for not keeping up.

It is important to recognise that no team, whether it consists of two people or two thousand, will work in harmony and at the same pace at all times. Only through understanding, that is, sympathy with the challenges the other is facing, will you achieve progress or if necessary release the other from a burden. Sympathy means kindness. Above all, do not feel that you are the victim of changes in the other; you will begin to feel inadequacy, self-pity and blame. These three together move downwards in an emotional vortex.

Instead have patience. Accept that so long as two people, or two teams, or two countries are working together with the same end in view, you will eventually come together as one. There will be disagreements, for just as reasoned argument sparks ideas, so conflict sparks invention and progress. If there is to be balance and co-operation, both sides must be satisfied that your creation is making headway. This means that each side has to be willing to make concessions: to take a small step back in order to take a big step forward.

Out of many small reconciliations and new beginnings you will create partnerships, loving unions and friendships. You will resolve conflicts, end rivalries, sign contracts and make treaties. In the end, all parties will win.

17 Emotional causes of disease

On being stuck

Very few people ever got sick from expressing emotions, but many illnesses are caused by suppressing them.

You know how it feels. In your thoughts, you constantly revisit events that caused you psychological pain. You are preoccupied with conversations or insults or actions that hurt you. You cannot move on: you want revenge, you wish you had done or said something else, or you want to express how much damage someone or something has done to you. You act out the trenchant response you wish you'd made, or you write devastatingly critical letters in your head, or you talk to everyone you meet about your grievance. Your mental condition is at best distracted, at worst obsessive. You're stuck.

Or maybe you have no problem with the past, although ahead of you lie two options, neither of them very attractive. You can do one thing and feel bad about it, or do nothing and feel worse. You try not to think about it; you hope the problem will go away. It doesn't. Since you can't deal with the anxiety, you can make no decision. You vacillate, and end up doing nothing about anything; every other small choice in your life is put on hold because you can't make decisions about the big things. Opportunities pass you by. You get more anxious because unless you do something soon, it will be too late. Again, you're stuck.

Your daily life is not moving forward as it should because you are emotionally screwed up, and you're not taking any notice of your body. This is when things start to go wrong.

Pain as a diversion

Any disease that cannot be traced to some kind of physical intrusion is the product of your emotional state. As soon as this becomes problematic, you will be susceptible to illness. You may blame some physical chain of events, but when you examine your emotional state you will admit your deeper awareness that unresolved problems underlie your pain. The pain is a diversion.

Emotions have a biochemical impact. In a tense emotional state when emotions are being suppressed, your mind is full of unresolved doubt. You must consciously face the present state of affairs and find the strength to overcome your difficulties. If you do not, you are choosing to live with a constant low level of anxiety, which means you will submit to physical weakness and deterioration.

If you are in the habit of interrogating your mind, you will be well placed to resolve your emotional issues; if you habitually live in denial of your inner emotions, you will be vulnerable to one illness after another.

Often these diseases have a superficial physical cause. You will look for this first; the parcel you were lifting when 'your back went', the washing powder that caused the rash, the cinema trip where you 'caught' a sore throat and your voice disappeared. Or maybe 'it's in the family.' You have inherited weak ankles (which is why yours is sprained) or high blood pressure, or your whole family has a tendency to suffer from chesty coughs. Instead of seeing yourself as the triumphant outcome of thousands of genetic winners (which historically you are) you imagine you are the victim of your family's medical history.

At other times, the conventional diagnosis is 'psychosomatic illness'. People who are not suffering may think this means you're making it up. This is not the case: your pain is certainly real and may even have been triggered by some minor physical accident or infection. But the reason you were susceptible in the first place is essentially emotional. Unfortunately, you do not know your own mind well enough to confront your emotions and deal with them.

You may find you have a particular weakness: your skin, your breathing, your blood pressure. Think about it and you recognise that it has only ever been a problem at difficult times: when you did your exams, when your partner was unfaithful, after the car accident. The reasons why you should be vulnerable to one weakness rather than another are often buried deep in your memory. Perhaps at some time a doctor, a parent or a friend has emphasised that a certain symptom will prove debilitating. This is the symptom you exhibit.

It starts like this. At a time of fear or negativity, you start to suffer from shortness of breath and panic attacks, or you sprain your ankle yet again, or you come out in a rash. The problem now becomes breathlessness, or the sprained ankle, or the rash; the emotional problem is pushed into the background.

This is all very well as long as you are suffering disease with a label, but once it fails to get better, or keeps recurring, and is labelled 'psychosomatic', or caused by 'stress', then you feel undermined. The legitimacy of your problem will be questioned, first because psychosomatic or stress-related illnesses are popularly seen as a sign of weakness, and secondly because no solution is offered. Nobody can offer a quick cure for stress or psychosomatic illness.

Now you start to create deeper fears and uncertainties. You can't work, you need to be looked after, you need to seek help. No work means financial difficulties, your partner cannot care for you so you quarrel, you seek help and the doctor's solution is useless. Your life is getting worse and the 'stress level' even higher. Your imagination takes over; you become depressed.

Your problems are making you miserable and the more miserable you feel, the more you alienate those around you. You can see no escape: you imagine that the only outcome is death. People can drive themselves to suicide this way.

Your illness has become your excuse for inadequacy. The world may accept it as such and this may make you miserable, but in fact it *provides the excuse you wanted*, because before the illness manifested itself, there were issues in your personal or professional life you didn't want to face.

Only you are in a position to be honest with yourself. Only you can say with any accuracy what was going on in your *emotional* life at the point when your symptoms first presented themselves. Once you have taken action to remove the causes of emotional conflict, you will start to get better.

Suggestibility

If you have the misfortune to be diagnosed with a known disease and are told that you will inevitably die within a short time, then if you are in an emotionally weakened state you will probably do exactly that. Your system takes instructions if you let it. This is self-evident: people perform astonishing feats of strength and daring in moments of crisis because they know they must, but equally they programme themselves to give up entirely if they 'know' that a disease is stronger than they are. They make an emotional decision.

In every case it is sensible to examine whose opinion is being believed. A prognosis of death or deterioration is, after all, only an opinion. It is not written in some supernatural book of the future. Well-informed medical professionals can base their opinion on your physical and biochemical state, but it is not their job to diagnose your emotional state or its possible effect on your recovery. Only you are in a position to diagnose your true emotional condition.

Remember that while doctors can help your body, you will

never be entirely well until your mind is at peace. It is up to you to deal with your emotional state. When you are ill, be particularly aware of the side-effects which certain curative drugs may be having on your emotions. You will probably be forewarned about the effects of the drugs you are expected to take, and these warnings must be taken seriously..

Proportion

You need to examine, not only the emotional trigger of your pain, but the deep-seated meaning that it has for you. Like everyone else, you are probably brave in the face of some misfortunes but brought low by others. Some people, for instance, can take sexual rejection in their stride but would feel suicidal at the loss of their personal wealth. Others would literally rather die than be divorced, but are perfectly happy to be seen driving around in an old car. Or maybe you feel you have failed someone in some respect, while in fact they never expected any help from you. Examine what your personal values and expectations are. Don't worry about who or what gave you these values, or waste time blaming your father or your maths teacher. Just reduce negative influences to their correct proportion.

Be open to suggestion: at times other people may put forward ideas which might help you. It is hard to look at such suggestions objectively if you are at a low point in your life, because you may read an implicit criticism into them. But do not snap at those who care for you: accept that these ideas are meant in good faith, with a helpful spirit, and if you listen and give thanks, they may one day inspire you to set off on the right path. It is not always easy to take radical steps without some encouragement or input from others.

If you find change threatening, your fear of the unknown, left examined, will make you anxious and depressed. Yet the unknown is not necessarily worse: it often turns out to be an improvement on the familiar. Depression always begins with emotional imbalance, and suppressing fear gives disease a chance to take hold, so confront your fears, examine them, and you will find that the worst that can happen, handled well, is not unbearable and may even be for the best.

Once you have decided what matters most to you, you will need to use strength of will to put it into proportion. Perhaps your values were impressed upon you when you were very young. Since you are now an adult, you know that life is much more complicated than you understood when you were a child. Nonetheless the voices of your parents may resonate in your mind to this day, telling you what is right and wrong. Think about those voices of authority. Think about being unable to live up to everything they demand. Would it really be so terrible? Do other perfectly well-adjusted people seem to have happy lives while being less than perfect according to the rules laid down for you, personally, in your childhood? If so, concede that your values and wants may have to be adjusted, at least temporarily, if you are to move forward and be happy. This will take strength of will, but once you let go of some demands, you will feel a burden lifting.

You are, in many ways, more fortunate than previous generations of your family. If you know the physical weaknesses they are known to have suffered from, you can ask yourself what emotional turmoil they may have had to live with. In past centuries and other places, rules were strict, and often communities were small and tight-knit and outside influences few. You live in an age (and probably a place) where options are open to you. You do not have to subscribe to the social norms of the past or of a tiny village; if your mother and grandmother and great-grandmother, back into the mists of time, suffered from depressive illness from the age of forty, there is no reason why you should. Your life is different, you have more control, and the choices open to you are different. Unless you live in an extremely restrictive religious community, you can do as you wish and not be ostracised; the opportunity is open to you to be care-*free.* You simply have to seize your opportunities and know your own mind.

Emotional resilience

The world we live in has always been threatening; there has been no time in human history when people have lived without fear of wild animals, unpredictable epidemics, natural disasters or capricious rulers. Now that we in the industrialised countries no longer fear these things, we live with new threats. We may, we are told, carry ourselves off to an early grave by by eating and drinking too much of the wrong things, by smoking and taking no exercise. No doubt this is all perfectly true, but you may know weaker-minded individuals who are terrified by warnings, believe themselves condemned, and become obsessively guilty because they eat 'forbidden' food or don't go to the gym.

Worse still, you may know people who cannot face life without drink or drugs to comfort them and give them courage. If you are one of these people, admit it: you are taking a serious risk. Consider the emotional and social background to your addiction. You and your friends may think it's okay to boast of your high alcohol or cocaine consumption. Be aware that yours is an antisocial boast. Or maybe you use prescribed medication, have been prescribed it for years, and resist reducing your dose because over time, as the original problem disappeared the medication itself replaced it and became your focus in life.

You know that an emotionally balanced life would almost certainly be preferable to one polluted by long-term medication or illicit drug use, but you are frightened to walk through life without a crutch. The results of addiction are well known to all of us, and never pretty; they hurt you and those around you. But you do not listen to your mind, which is strong. Instead, you develop an emotional conviction that you are too weak to deal with life by yourself.

Where do you get this idea? It is true that by using the crutch all the time, you weaken your own powers of resilience; you do become more emotionally volatile, not less. But if you have the courage to instruct your mind to exercise its good sense in your own interests and ignore the physical manifestations of your dependency, you will recover.

Often, because you are confused, one idea keeps returning to throw you off balance. Be resilient: ignore that idea. Ask yourself 'What does it matter?' Ask yourself 'What does anything matter if I have health and strength with which to deal with problems in the way I know in my mind to be right?' Because that is the real question, and the one which will give you the confidence to *take action* instead of falling prey to anxiety and depression. If you take care of your emotional health, then your mind will take care of you.

18 Dependency

Loss of confidence

Confidence is what drives you. You feel confident enough to assert yourself, and everyone you encounter must have confidence in you.

Yet in a complex world, your confidence is challenged all the time by new ideas and the need to acquire new skills and meet new people. This may make you feel uncertain of yourself, and negative, and timid. If so, this is an opportunity for dependence and addiction to take hold.

A small example: perhaps you are at a party, and have a drink. You need more confidence than usual to make your presence felt, so you have a second drink. You may think you are oiling the social wheels, but what you are focussing on is having a drink. After a few more you don't want to stop: you are drunk. Your behaviour has changed and you no longer care what other people think of you.

If you do this often enough, it becomes a habit. Pretty soon you can't imagine functioning in public without alcohol; the drink has come to dominate your idea of what parties, or in fact any social gathering, are about. As the habit is now part of who you are, you are dependent.

If you persist in drinking, you first lose your reason. You are no longer capable of looking after yourself and you may attack others. Next your brain shuts your mind and body down. You lose control; your body shuts down to protect you, and if you are fortunate, this will happen when you are out of harm's way. If you are not, you might pass out on the edge of a canal or at the wheel of a car.

This is escapism beyond reason, with grave consequences. Yet inside you there must be the confidence just to be *who you are*. If you drink to try to be someone else, you make yourself no better than a slave.

Alienation

You may have experienced alienation. Perhaps you have found yourself in conflict with your family or lonely in a strange new community. You begin to question the integrity or opinions or habits of the people around you. You know you don't want to be part of what they stand for, but they seem uncomprehending and show no sign of wanting to change.

This is frustrating. You are determined to assert yourself. In fact you want all these others to listen, take notice, be shocked into recognition that you have different and better rules to live by. If you were able to pick and choose some of their ideas and mix them with your own and discuss these things, you might not feel so alienated – but you can't; you're angry and they seem so smug. So you withdraw as far as you can.

You can withdraw furthest inside your own head. No-one can get to you there. And if you take mind-altering drugs, for instance, stimulant or tranquillising or hallucinatory drugs which may include alcohol, you can persuade yourself that your withdrawal itself is a kind of triumph. You enjoy yourself at last, and you convince yourself that your inner journey is teaching you a higher truth. Your identity now becomes bound up with your idea of yourself as someone in possession of secret information and a superior kind of experience and a more daring attitude to life. Instead of being frustrated by your alienation, you actively enjoy it.

However, you need to stay in that state of mind. The effects wear off, usually leaving you feeling a lot worse than before, so you need to take your drug of choice all over again. Eventually a physical addiction begins, and when it does, craving becomes painful.

None of this is necessary. Instead of withdrawing from the world into the dead end of dependency, you can withdraw from it into your mind, and work out how to use your talents for your own good. In your mind, you can be released from tension and pain and regain confidence through understanding. Your journeys into to your mind will heal you.

Repression

You may bottle up fears, or flights of fancy, or your own inadequacies. You may refuse to admit what you really want or the kind of person you really are or the jealousy and dislike that really drives you. All these repressions, and many others, must have a kind of psychological safety valve – often self-indulgence. This may mean drugs and alcohol but it could mean food or sex.

It can even mean shopping. One particularly dangerous kind of shopping is buying pills and other means of self-medication, over the counter. So interesting does the purchase of a new cure become that the self-medication addict will readily dream up a symptom, and suffer it, in order to provide a reason for taking a pill. This is a psychosomatic illness of a particularly self-indulgent kind, and the payoff is 'Be good to yourself,' silently whispered as the drug is ingested.

The more cunning self-medicator prefers to act the part of sick person, thereby getting, not just the prescribed-medicine payoff, but also the pleasure of being taken seriously by a figure of authority, usually a doctor. These prescribed drugs are, of course, official, and therefore come pure and polished with extra status. Those who take them feel superior to those who take alternative medications or recreational drugs, nicotine or alcohol.

Dependency should not be misinterpreted as mere comfort-seeking; it is more serious than that, and the only person who will lose by it is yourself. If you dose yourself with substances that alter your mood or your consciousness in any way, you are more likely to escape your problems than to deal with them. For a short time your drugs will lighten your burden, but in the longer term, they will make matters worse.

Instead be inquisitive: examine what you are repressing, and give your mind time to give you an answer. What you learn should remain sacred to you alone. Don't talk about the process of self-examination, for if you do you will start to do it self-consciously, with the feeling that you have an audience waiting for the next revelation. Respect your own privacy, and be prepared for the inward journey to take a long time.

Avoidance

Dependencies of all kinds are a kind of avoidance – ways of refusing to confront life and the people in it; ways of refusing to confront your own mind.

Who am I? What am I doing here? What is my purpose? Where am I going? How do I know if this is right for me? These are difficult questions and if you are not in touch with your mind, they will leave you confused and fearful. The tests of life will be too much for you.

Yet none of life's tests are to be avoided, because they serve a purpose. They all help to educate your consciousness to achieve insight. The more you remain open to everything around you, the more acutely aware you will be of small changes that may affect your destiny. Lessons in life are all around you, every day, and together they teach you how to walk on the right path. You cannot know this unless you stay alert. If you spend your waking life in the search for comfort in a bottle or a syringe or a fridge full of food, all life's lessons are wasted on you; you are stuck, and cannot make progress.

All your experiences, the highs and the lows, are blessings however intolerable they may sometimes seem. They shape your perceptions and prepare you for further experiences and bring you closer to your destiny; your task is simply to remain alert, and exercise your capacity to learn, for your mind will absorb all you know at the deepest level, and your memories and knowledge will be available to you in the future.

Status

Without realising it, you can be psychologically dependent on your own status. You fall apart when suddenly you are no longer Chairman of the Board, or top of the class, or the most beautiful woman in the room. Your identity is out of balance, over-dependent on one aspect of yourself.

If you are rational, you will recognise that everything goes in cycles and it's someone else's turn: now you have to look elsewhere and start something new. Unfortunately, at the end of every cycle you may feel fearful as your mind prepares for changes ahead, and if you are over-dependent on your present station in life for a sense of identity, you will suffer. You will hope for a rescuer but in due course you must recognise that you are your own rescuer.

So although your withdrawal from dependence on your status may appear harsh, it will ultimately teach you to change your life for the best. Do not wallow in the sympathy of others; listen to your mind, because there is a purpose in your life and you must now make the correct choices and commit yourself to them.

19 The Healing Mind

Asthma

Asthma involves chronic episodes of breathlessness, or even inability to breathe. It is believed to be related to inflammation of the airways or allergies, but there are many possible causes. As nobody has yet come up with a single definition of what makes it happen, the symptoms are medically treatable but the ailment itself is not.

At the age of 18 I began experiencing shortness of breath and tightness in the chest. I was told I had asthma – a new label to add to the list of psychosomatic conditions from which I was already suffering. But this one came with a bonus: I had a toy. I enjoyed carrying it around. I lost my breath when I was with other people, and proudly produced My Inhaler. At the slightest suspicion of shortness of breath, I flourished my little blue gadget and felt relief.

I had asthma for about a year. When you are diagnosed as an asthmatic, and experience the illness, you start looking at other people, and you notice what they have in common. Even then, I suspected that my imagination and my emotions had an effect on my body. My experience helped me understand the way the condition worked.

Before I started my practice, a teenager who had suffered severe asthma attacks came to see me for help. When I explained how I thought asthma worked, she was cured. She forgot she'd ever had an asthma attack. For I had observed (and I'd told her) that asthma triggers itself at times of emotional upheaval. Emotional excitement can put you into a physical state in which your body becomes so tense that you forget to breathe out. This naturally causes tightness in the chest, as you can't breathe in.

Asthma develops. It starts and gets worse, but only rarely becomes life-threatening. Nonetheless asthma attacks are extremely traumatic; if you've never experienced such a thing, imagine being suffocated. It's like dying – the whole of your past life flashes past. These thoughts and images come thick and so fast that the physical reaction alone is all-consuming. Your body is out of control and your emotions take over.

So it is important to be aware of your breathing patterns. If you are to deal with asthmatic episodes, you must bring balance to your body and mind. Ensure that you breathe out before you try breathing in. Breathe in and out through your mouth, and you will absorb the energy to achieve that balance.

As for your imagination, when you begin to practise breathing you must control your imagination by breathing in through the nose and our through your mouth. Focus on your mind.

Elation, excitement, extreme sadness and emotional volatility can literally take your breath away. Whenever you can, avoid extremes of emotion. How can you do this? By avoiding what is socially expected; by knowing your own mind; by giving in to emotion when you must, but always knowing that this moment is not the end – after the grief, the joy, are over, there will be other moments.

Over-breathing will not work for you unless your breathing is goal-directed. Breathe naturally and in a relaxed way. You know that your mind is your master and will carry out all your instructions effectively. Never attempt to hold your breath. Your mind can restrain any threat to your body, but you must control the depth and timing of your breathing.

The technique may take some time to master, but once mastered not only will it return you to your natural fearless state, but it will eliminate similar weaknesses – such as any so-called psychosomatic ailments.

Autism

If your child is autistic, you'll know that any attempt to inspire an interest in something they're uninterested in in the first place is impossible. Regular 'training' of a conventional kind is for this reason out of the question. Their minds register what is important to them and reject the rest. They easily become bored, frustrated and unruly if they are asked to learn something – yet they can focus intensely on what captures their attention from moment to moment. It's important to keep autistic children stimulated, so that they can explore the full range of possible ways to express themselves.

Autistic individuals may puzzle us with their behaviour, such as repeating the same action over and over again. Often they find it impossible to show emotion, but they can find balance, learn to use their unconscious memory effectively and contribute a great deal to our understanding of life.

The pent-up emotion they don't express can be interpreted as a kind of freedom, or alternatively as the cause of stress. The important thing is to find one's own balance in dealing with the autistic individual; on the one hand to leave them free to approach life on their own terms, on the other to make life easier for them by encouraging their abilities to blossom. You'll need to find the level of discipline that's right for that particular individual.

You'll find that when you try a soft approach you won't be listened to, but don't reprimand or enforce your will as this causes chaos and confusion as well as retaliation. If, however, you simply make a strong statement in a strong voice, you will get a reaction deep in the mind. You can retrain an autistic mind by applying the kind of discipline that helps the young person feel good about their own abilities and motivates them to reach more ambitious long-term goals.

Autism itself is testimony to the power of the mind.

Dyslexia

To deal positively with dyslexia you will need intense focus and conscious mental coordination.

You're probably 'dyslexic' in at least one area – you probably think of it as your blind spot; the one thing that makes your eyes glaze over; the one thing you just never get right. Does this make you inadequate? Of course not; none of us can be expected to perform well in all areas of endeavour, but the things that capture our imagination are those we do best at. Dyslexics are found in every walk of life and in this respect they're just like the rest of us, only more so. They find it difficult to concentrate on subjects that require a disciplined approach to learning unless they are motivated by strong interest. They tend to rely on creative ability and are often celebrated as entrepreneurs.

If you are the parent of a dyslexic child, remember their innovative gifts are valuable, so encourage them in all they do. With support and guidance they will do well. There is no point in trying to force them to conform to academic expectations, as this may undermine their confidence.They may seem to be slow learners, but the wider their range of experience, and the more freedom they are given to to express themselves, the more self-confident they will get.

ME (myalgic encephalopathy)

This is also called *chronic fatigue syndrome*; sufferers, usually young, begin to weaken and tire without any given reason, and in my experience they also get anxiety and panic attacks. Other effects vary from person to person. Some have allergic reactions, some exhibit physical symptoms, and others can't sleep. Although this is a *fatigue* syndrome, the fatigue itself is not the illness. Deadening fatigue is just the symptom, but it happens without any extraordinary physical exertion. None of the people who have approached me have led particularly active lives, although in theory they were physically fit enough. Their greatest strength was exercising their creativity: that is, their minds.

Besides this, I have always found that sufferers are influenced by a domineering presence; either a parent or some other figure of authority who imposes control on every aspect of their being. This controlling behaviour affects emotions, implying that the individual is powerless to the point of submission.

I believe that these young people, without consciously deciding to do so, are trying to get in touch with their own minds. To do so means detaching oneself from the environment – acting in a kind of waking dream, in full awareness of the imaginative journey you're on. Mental activity of this kind is tiring – physically tiring – which is why, if the mind is struggling, the result will be interpreted as exhaustion.

If you feel inadequate and emotionally negative because you feel crushed by a dominant authority, you can easily become vulnerable to a downward spiral of negative recollections, resentments and worries. You feel alienated and lose the will to carry on with life as it is; you have no idea how to organise an alternative way of being, but your body shuts down so that you have time to think.

You are stuck in a pattern of behaviour, but the perceptions that others have of you, and the way they behave towards you, are stuck too. If you don't cut the strings that bind you, you will find these patterns extremely hard to change. You know this, but you may try to suppress the knowledge. If you do, your symptoms can become paralysing or manifest themselves in other bodily complications.

I have helped ME sufferers by treating them with words. Words seem to alter their attitude towards getting better. Our minds perceive words at a very deep level, and sounds can alter our state of consciousness and induce activity or inactivity in all of us. When the mind sees the possibility of a breakthrough, I believe it alters the brain's chemical balance in such a way that instructions seem to get through: the person who has been chronically inert, having *seen what to do,* suddenly feels stronger and able to take action. Transformation can happen with astonishing speed, once the initial step has been taken. The damaging state is halted and then thrown into reverse as the sufferer once more starts to take control.

When you feel this moment has been reached, reward your own mind by applying reason to the emotional situation you must leave. This may mean practical upheavals, and you will have to be strong to face them. You must train to use your mind effectively so that you are no longer vulnerable at any time.

Remember that the past cannot be changed. It is your past, despite all its problems, that has brought you to this positive point, where you can take power over your own life because you can listen to your own mind. From now on can transform weaknesses to strengths because your imagination and creativity are yours to control. They will no longer be used to undermine and torture you, but to make you strong.

Medication

The ME sufferer's mind is in search of answers, rather than medication. Tranquillisers can make matters worse, while stimulants have no beneficial effect since it is your mind that is restricted, not your body. You may become physically more active, but it's only the symptom that's being treated; no drug can effect a cure.

There are daily practical exercises to do which will help your recovery better than any pills.

Walking

Breathe in and out through your mouth.

Your breathing should be slow and deep. This will supply oxygen to the blood and help your muscles.

Prepare to walk. If you have been restricted physically then exercise at home at first. Don't just walk aimlessly; decide on a goal.

Instruct your mind: you are walking towards a goal.

Moving towards an objective will unlock your suppressed will.

Breathe deeply in through your nose. Now you are increasing the flow of oxygen to your brain.

Instruct your mind; you are about to walk to another goal.

I have worked with a person who, having been confined to a few rooms for five years, was able after ten minutes of mind instruction to walk a mile. This is the power of mind instruction. It shows how simply negative thought patterns can be changed once the *will* has been engaged.

Writing

The first flash of insight into your true situation is the most important moment in your progress. You will certainly be helped if you start to write the issues down. Don't make judgements about anything. Just list what could be wrong and quite soon, messages will begin to surface from the depths of your mind. If you get carried away with writing, and later read what you've written, you may be amazed at how much you really understood your situation all along; but until you began to write, your conscious mind had no channel through which to acknowledge much that was important but painful.

Balance

If you are the kind of imaginative individual who is most vulnerable to ME, you will need to maintain a peaceful state of mind if you are to resist recurrent attacks. Your natural wisdom and creativity must be accessible at all times, because there will be times when other people attempt to inflict emotional damage.

Deportment

Your back and stomach are two most sensitive areas, and either can suffer when you have had ME. It is important for both that your posture is correct.

Stand upright with eyes closed

Breathe in through your nose.

You feel lighter. Breathe into your whole body so that energy flows freely.

Sleep

If your sleeping patterns are distorted, your mind is predisposed to confusion and your body is weakened. Make every effort to get up early and go to bed well before midnight.

Lie down in a warm bed and switch out the light. Feel your body relax.

Practise slowly breathing in and out through the mouth.

Focus on your mind. Imagine there's a dark screen in your forehead and it holds tranquillising patterns for your mind to watch.

You are going to sleep now; the patterns appear and disappear and are replaced; this is your mind's sacred time and no thought is allowed to intrude.

MND (motor neurone disease and related disorders)

Motor neurone disease is a neurological disorder which affects certain neurones in the brain and spinal cord. These are the neurones that would normally send messages to the muscles via electrical impulses. With motor neurone disruption, the muscles are left inert and start to waste away.

It can begin gradually, with muscle weakness. Your hands and fingers feel weak and you find it hard to grip. Even lifting your foot to put one in front of another gets difficult. Sometimes swallowing and speaking cause distress, or your muscles start to twitch. There are variations of all these, and variations of degree, but since MND looks rather like a number of other things in the early stages, it is difficult to diagnose at the outset. Sometimes limbs are affected, sometimes throat and facial muscles and speech. The degree to which people become ill, and the disease's rate of progression, differ immensely, and you can be affected at any age from twenty to seventy.

I have observed that symptoms first occur in consequence of some apparently minor emotional trigger. Emotions play a significant role in the progress of this disease, and recovery is often inhibited by painful thoughts, rooted in the traumas of the past, forcing themselves to the surface.

What matters is to remove emotional *authority* over the symptoms.

I have also observed that people with motor neurone disease are of a certain type: at times they are extremely gentle, timid and kind, but they can also be over-energetic and then it's as if they are powered by aggression.

The condition is widely associated with people who are involved in competitive sport. This of course offers a scenario for a battle between weak and strong which is reflected in the individual's mind, brain and body. Such energies are not exerted in a balanced way and extremes of strength can suddenly collapse into weakness.

Quite why people suffer from MND, nobody knows; among areas of research are genetic inheritance, cell mechanisms that cause motor neurones to deteriorate, environmental factors, viruses and parasites. Medical specialists consider that it is incurable and there is no hope of recovery or remission. They often describe symptoms that will occur one after another with grim inevitability until early death results. This kind of prognosis is tantamount to a death sentence, and few minds are strong enough to resist interpreting it as a command.

In the past, MND seemed usually to strike in middle

age, but younger people are getting it now. And fear is part of it. A minute spasm occurs and this weakens the limbs; it's frightening.

Ultimately the weakness begins to spread, just as your doctor said it would. This is the most frightening thing of all. If your doctor said you would lose control of the muscles in your throat and you could choke to death, you feel like choking soon you've heard this awful prognosis. Your speech becomes slurred; swallowing is hard; your mouth and face feel numb; your tongue feels heavy and breathing is difficult. Since you're inhaling insufficient air, you move more slowly.

When I have been fortunate enough to encounter MND sufferers at this early stage (not long after they started to lose the power of speech) I have been able to teach them to regain control over their own minds. They get their confidence back, and start to speak normally in a relatively short space of time. Those who have lost their speech completely can be helped, although they may not return to complete normality, and for some the degree of effort required has proved too onerous.

The dire prognoses pronounced by too many specialists have such a fearful effect that the vulnerable may never recover. The prospect of a lingering death can prove impossible to eradicate. My success in managing to halt the symptoms and spread of the condition is more likely when diagnosis is recent and the patient resistant to medical opinion or suspicious of it. In no case should a person interpret medical opinion as medical decree. If they do, it will of course lead to inert acceptance followed by too-rapid deterioration.

As MND is a muscle-wasting condition it is imperative to exercise limbs, face and throat to counteract loss of muscle mass. The regenerative capacity of connections between brain and muscle is not understood, but in the absence of a neurone repair pill, exercise is surprisingly effective. Those who take instructions seriously, work hard and maintain a strenous level of activity in their daily lives do manage to control deterioration and even restore mobility. The 'flickering' of muscles ceases. Limbs previously pronounced useless become stronger and perform normally; hands with no control or grip start to function normally, although hand and arm movement takes longest to stabilise.

Persistence

The results that I have seen leave me in no doubt that this condition can be controlled, although my treatment has a particular pitfall: optimism. Because people come to me hopeless and suddenly recognise that they can help themselves, they defy fear and become elated. Believing that they can control the illness if they so choose, they treat it with careless abandon and start to deteriorate fast. This will not do; *wasted* muscles will be very hard to restore to anything like normality. The disease is real and has to be fought daily, literally every step of the way, with will power and exercise. Those who recognise this return time and again for guidance and encouragement and are able to maintain control.

Balance

Your mind must be the starting point for recovery, that is, the analysis, control and alteration of emotional perceptions to bring your mind, body and brain into balance. As you undertake physical exercise, you will need to co-ordinate the energies that control your movement. Stop being nervous about what may happen to your body, and recognise the control that your mind can direct to your brain and the potential your brain still has for helping you recuperate. Remember that you alone possess the power to reverse this condition and halt its progress, and you will do this through a balanced exercise plan.

When you are at rest you cannot build muscle mass; however, you need also to avoid over-exercise and fatigue. Exercise gently, breathing deeply. Do all the things you have always done: walk, get up and sit down, carry out your daily tasks and talk as much as you can. Read aloud and practise difficult pronunciation. When circumstances are such that you must remain still, silently tense and relax your muscles.

You may find yourself making more physical effort than usual but it's important to do so; you are instructing your brain to maintain connections.

Control

All past resentments and self-inflicted fears and anxieties must be seen as they are: redundant. Throw them out. Emotional stresses will harm you. Your own mental strength must dominate your thoughts. Pay attention to your posture and movement and the ease with which you can move your body. Your increased mobility will be apparent to everyone, but the important key to it all – control and focus by your mind – is for you alone to assess and improve.

Nutrition

Food intake must increase; eat small amounts frequently throughout the day. It may be a good idea to concentrate on organic produce. I have seen no improvements from exclusion diets and suspect that depriving yourself of particular food groups may be unhelpful. After all, your brain needs food too.

And it is because your brain needs the best possible nutrition that alcohol, tobacco and other recreational drugs should not be used. These things deplete you of vitamins and will certainly change the chemical balance of your brain, and this is the last thing you want: your brain must be unimpeded by such interference if it is to combat neurone deterioration.

MS (multiple sclerosis)

MS sufferers have attended my clinic from the day I opened it, and I confess myself unable always to help. This is because I cannot reverse patterns of behaviour that have proved rewarding to the patient.

MS is a complex condition. The signs (lesions visible on tissue surrounding fibres in the central nervous system) can appear anywhere in the CNS; the symptoms vary in type and degree; and the progression of the disease also differs according to type.

As I am no diagnostician, I have had to work from the ill-effects backwards. People have told me they've suffered from progressively increasing weakness, first in their legs, slowly spreading upwards to their hands and arms. Often I have managed to increase their confidence and we've seen significant improvement quite quickly. Unfortunately, this has usually been followed by weakening and a refusal to continue the exercise programme.

I believe there is an emotional blockage here. If you don't demand that your body should move, it won't, and the muscles will deteriorate.

In one case, the individual had been in a wheelchair for three years and hadn't walked in all that time. She was slim but the muscle mass in her legs was still palpable. After her second session I prompted her to get up and walk. She took the Zimmer frame and did so, but then stopped, turned, stumbled hurriedly back to the wheelchair and sat down, disbelieving what she had just done.

The following week she refused to try. After about four more sessions, I prompted her once again and insisted that she got up and walked. This time she walked better, with more control, and further. As if in a state of shock from what she had achieved, she then sped amazingly fast back to her wheelchair and refused to get up again. From the moment that she found out that it was possible to make herself mobile, she never returned to see me.

I have had the same experience with numerous multiple sclerosis sufferers.

All of them have been highly creative and imaginative individuals, most with partners who serve them with great conviction and care, carrying out all the necessary chores, responding to their every demand graciously and calmly.

The patients have been aged from twenty-something to

sixty. I have noticed astonishing similarities in the way they conduct their affairs and see themselves.

There was a man in his fifties who had to be brought into my clinic on a stretcher from an ambulance. After a brief discussion and analysis I explained my views and findings about this disease. He began crying uncontrollably because, he said, he had at last found someone who understands how this condition works. His legs would not carry him at all; he had been bedridden. His arms and hands were healthy and strong; he said that he exercised his arms regularly.

When strength of that nature is present in one part of the body it is possible that other parts of the body are equally strong, but simply need guidance. On his second visit I persuaded him to arrive in a wheelchair and not on a stretcher. Laughingly I challenged him; I asked him to grab the climbing bars in my clinic and stand up, which he did. I made him repeat standing and sitting several times. He was excited – he could do it.

Soon afterwards, I sensed the novelty wearing off. He began to look thoughtful. I thought: *he won't do it again*. I was right. He was meant to come the following week but he didn't turn up. That thoughtful look had told me already: 'getting better' wasn't what he was looking for. Why that is, I'm not sure. I could guess that perhaps normality would be too dull. MS is real enough; there is no disputing that. But did the *extent* of his debility have something attention-seeking about it?

This same pattern continued with all individuals that I treated with this condition. I tried long and hard to understand the reason for it. With no disrespect, I have reached the conclusion that this is a lazy disease. Not that the individuals are lazy in all respects, as some work in high positions. They come from different backgrounds and nationalities. But there is a lack of drive, a disinterest. And there's also something deeper going on.

In certain cases they talked about childhood traumas that had made them feel inadequate. They felt guilty because their dreams could never come true and now they were no longer in a position to make them happen. As a sick person, they had everything done for them and had become used to telling their partners what to do. At the same time they all spoke about how they needed to recover, not for their own sake, but to lighten their partner's burden.

Multiple sclerosis is one of the simplest conditions to treat. People have no need to suffer, nor to spend their life in wheelchairs, nor to impose their will upon their loved ones. If we stop making allowances for them, and stop suggesting that they are weak and will get weaker, these people will continue to walk and will have no choice but to walk.

However, the need to recover must come from them, and not from other people. Some embark on a recovery programme only to pacify their nearest and dearest and promptly fail, or choose to. The partner who cares for them must now conclude that this condition is so debilitating that the patient needs constant, long-term attention.

I observed that in almost every case the caring partners had perceptions, attitudes and reactions in common with each other. They, like the patient, felt guilty, but for a different reason: they felt they couldn't do enough for this person. The weak patient dominated the strong carer by unconsciously inflicting guilt.

So long-term sufferers have not been among my successes. In cases that have been recently diagnosed, however, I have managed to eliminate the condition by explaining the way this psychological manipulation can work and instructing patients not to weaken but to resist. These individuals have become happy and healthy, and with their outlook no longer dominated by the conviction that they are weakening, their condition has improved.

There will always be a few people who welcome, at a deep level, an excuse to achieve nothing more. As this condition takes a long time to worsen, they are insufficiently aware of the damage they can do by sheer lack of will. If the disease is allowed to progress they become invalids out of habit, and simply cannot imagine how they would cope with normal life. This kind of habituation is not uncommon in any chronic illness, but with MS it is always marked.

Not only do their own ambitions and those of their partner remain unfulfilled, but their body really will suffer the effects of inertia. They must seize the initiative and work hard to get better.

Breathe
Breathe deeply in through your nose to bring life and energy to every part of your brain.

Focus
Focus on your mind. Your thoughts can empower your brain and your brain can empower your body. You will push yourself.

Accept
Acknowledge every improvement. Accept that each step you make will speed up recovery and healing.

Reject weakness
Until now you have made *emotional judgements* about your illness. If you interpret feelings of weakness as a warning to stop trying, you will remain weak. But if you apply yourself with the mind-set of a long-distance runner or Tour de France cyclist, you will ignore weariness, reject weakness, keep going no matter what, and improve, building muscle strength.

Accept
Accept that nothing can stand between you and your mind. Everything you need is there; you have only to look for it with passion, determination and persistence. Nothing shall weaken you for you possess a mind and an active brain. Your limbs are connected to your brain and your mind is your source of power. Accept that from now on, your imagination and your dreams will lead you to *action*.

Obsessive Compulsive Disorder (OCD)

Obsessive compulsives repeat actions out of anxiety just in case they didn't get it right the first time. If this is you, you will wash your hands again and again (they always feel dirty; your obsession is their dirtiness) or check and re-check the window locks (just in case) or align the table mats *precisely* and burst into tears if they're displaced. There are hundreds of variants on these common compulsions. Obsessions are usually accompanied by compulsions and I have come across some odd ones – such as the belief held by one of my patients that if he were to kiss a girl and their teeth touched, he would go to hell; or the lady who would nibble two-thirds of a biscuit but must then throw away the part touched by her own fingers.

Obsessions and compulsions sound comical until you recognise that they keep people stuck in a mental loop. It is as if an infection had set in and spread deep into your mind, contaminating rational thought. As a result, the ritualistic hand-washing or counting the words you speak or tidying up can consume so much of your time as to become disabling. You are unable to conduct normal life. Nothing happens; your needle is stuck in a groove, and you replay the same sequence of fears, ideas and movements again and again and again.

This inability to move forwards or backwards stems from some past failure to satisfy authority or deal with a situation. Whatever happened inflicted a feeling of inadequacy so painful that it must be avoided by constant effort forever. From now on there must be not a single iota of a jot of a whisper of a chance of getting life's table mats out of alignment.

No resolution is possible, since the problem is in your mind in the first place. Round and round the fears, ideas and movements come again, endlessly, as you avoid confronting those unpleasant emotions. It's like that torture technique in which you're driven mad by having water endlessly drip, drip onto your forehead.....

You'll need help if you're to return to a working relationship with the world. Family and friends, however well-meaning, inevitably provoke emotions, usually rebellious ones. A stranger with experience can usually make a successful intervention, and behaviour can change quickly if a patient is treated with kindness, the cause of the original false belief is brought into the open and the basic techniques of mind instruction are learned.

Once you learn to get in touch with your mind, interrogate your memories and identify the issues that created your compulsion you will recognise that the demands of other people are behind it. You are afraid of what other people – probably people who are no longer part of your life – once *threatened* to think, or what you thought they thought, or what they said they thought and then probably forgot.

Ask yourself why this ever mattered so much, and you may find you have no answer.

You have been trying to please someone who isn't there and cannot care.

In all the cases I've dealt with it, words of wisdom and logic were all that was required for the person to understand and feel released from their obsession. Once one conclusion was drawn, the whole pattern of compulsive behaviour fell apart like a house of cards.

Once you have learned to reach the power of your own mind and use it resourcefully you will never again suffer from compulsions. You will no longer suppress unpleasant emotions; why should you? You now respect your own mind and your capacity to resist pressure from other people. Should you falter, you can trust your own will to restore your balance. Trust the creativity and insight of your own mind; only your mind can bring peace to you, for it is your master and has a journey to complete.

Parkinson's disease

Parkinson's is sometimes knoawn as the 'stop and go' disease, because it brings with it a tendency to hesitation and repetitiveness. I have worked with many Parkinson's discase sufferers and without exception, these have been inspiring experiences.

I have seen people with highly creative minds whose brains visibly repeat themselves in instructing the body, returning to same starting point in a given action and never reaching completion. Their imagination seems to accelerate to such a level that they get stuck in a loop and their brains make them go down the same route over and over again. This particularly affects mobility, which can suddenly stop – triggered, for no apparent reason, by something as minor as a threshold to cross or a corner to turn.

One 75 year-old man who came to see me struggled to walk into the room, then struggled to stand up from his seat and completely lost his balance. He tried to manoeuvre himself around his chair and could not move. I gave him instructions and within five minutes, negotiating tight corners was no longer a problem; nor was facing a wall; and he managed to manoeuvre himself out of his situation.

Your body's behaviour reflects the working of your mind. In Parkinson's, the shaking and hesitation and feeling of being 'stuck' are all signs of fear or guilt. We all have fears and guilts, but the Parkinson's sufferer has to ignore these emotions entirely. They turn into obsessive nervousness and a horrid mental vortex; the fear of the symptom is enough to trigger it, and with every episode the nervousnessness worsens.

There is an inner drive, an inner energy that makes this condition unique. If you have Parkinson's you may well feel healthy, although you sometimes tremble for no apparent reason.

All the people I have seen still have strong muscles; almost none of them have been taking medication. There was just one individual who was on extremely high doses of drugs. He took a tablet every thirty minutes, a strong drug in the morning and another in the evening. He was ambulant, but to me he seemed practically comatose: he could not open his eyes or even speak to answer questions. When I read the possible side-effects of the medication he was taking I was horrified. His sense of his own presence seemed to be completely destroyed; he had turned into a walking zombie.

Over three months of consultation, improvement was significant. He came off all his medication, his eyes opened, he became alert and would laugh and joke with me. He had new ideas about business. This human being, who had appeared in my clinic like one of the walking dead, was alive and full of surprises. He could once again write perfectly and had long periods of thinking normally. All the same, the nightmares and hallucinations inflicted by the medication were difficult to erase from his memory.

If I had only actions and behaviour to go on, I would conclude that Parkinson's is a form of obsessive compulsive disorder. That's what it looks like. It is of course far stronger and less resistible, but it works in the same way; like OCD sufferers, people with Parkinson's have the ability to think, but an inability to *do*. With Parkinson's, the motivational stage of instruction from brain to muscle is made with such difficulty that the repeated actions are all false starts.

If you are a sufferer, you may often feel isolated and detached from life; you'll feel spaced out, then you'll come back down to earth, and feel grounded again. And this mental state, too, keeps recurring.

Sometimes you may get the impression that you're actively selecting situations or people that trigger these symptoms. If instances recur, then this hesitant, frustratingly repetitious behaviour will spread to all areas of life. So if you aim to alleviate or halt this condition, decide always to question *why* you should react to any situation in the way that you do now.

Explore your feelings and fearlessly demand that your unconscious mind should make a change in your behaviour.

Do not fear uncertainty. There are no uncertainties to fear. Have courage instead.

If Parkinson's disease is caught in its early stages it is easy to alter your thought processes so as to transform behaviour, avoid deterioration and halt the condition in its tracks. If you practise deep breathing and focussed concentration of the mind, it seems possible to alter the messages which your brain is sending to your body.

Instructions

The moment you feel you are about to hesitate, *focus on your mind.*

Breathe *in* deeply though your nose.

Now you are concentrating on an action, not an emotion.

Practise this until you can do it. Practise, especially, breathing with focus into the calm essence of your mind. If you find you are stuck in an action, simply try again, focussing on your mind, rather than your body.

As soon as you feel the slightest improvement, work even harder. Always acknowledge these changes to yourself; your mind will only respond if you instruct it to do what you want, and you must consciously want it to reach a desired level.

Your mind can return your body to its original healthy state. At first some slight weakness may remain because it is in the nature of your consciousness to feel doubtful; ignore this and keep going. Remember it is not only the emotional accumulation of a lifetime that triggers this condition, but also your culturally acquired acceptance of disease as something that 'can't be helped', that you've got to 'live with'. In fact resistance is possible with long-term application of an exercise regimen and persistent, focussed control of the mind.

Spinal cord injury

In theory, when the spinal cord is severed, damaged or compressed the result is complete and irremediable paralysis because the impulses that create momentum are physically blocked. In practice, some mobility can be restored.

If you apply your imagination and will-power effectively and refuse to be downhearted or negative, you will succeed. I have seen this happen with so many people that I *know* strong motivation can effect an improvement. Either the brain is diverting the mind's commands via some alternative route, or it is making the best use of the few neurones that remain; whatever is going on physically, if you have this kind of injury, the will to mobilise your limbs must come from your mind.

'Improvement' applies, too, to those who accept that they will remain paralysed. They have achieved a kind of peace; now they need to improve their quality of life. They often approach me because they are depressed. As they will always miss the mentally beneficial effects of healthy exercise, they need to learn techniques for dealing with depression and understanding the world, and their disability, from a healthier perspective.

Mobility

How is it that so many spinal cord injury patients are less mobile than they could be? Able-bodied people don't even think about how they get about in the course of an ordinary day, but just do it. Then they have an accident, and when they're at their most vulnerable a figure of authority – a doctor – announces 'you will never walk again'. This is deeply affecting. It's the sort of statement you don't forget. It causes a real mental wound that doesn't heal and you have to be strong-willed to question it, especially since this sentence is usually pronounced when you're at your lowest ebb.

I am convinced that the shock of such prognoses can make your mind shut down its communication with your brain.

After that, you don't really try; the whole idea of putting one foot in front of the other becomes a distant memory. The prognosis has fulfilled itself; the paralysis is evident, therefore you conclude that it must be permanent, and lose the will even to try to move.

If you refuse to accept paralysis from the start you have the best chance of regaining sensation and partial control. You still remember how to move, and because you refuse to be negative, you encourage your own will power. So recent habit, and a good attitude, keep your mind active and connections open.

If your spinal cord was injured years ago and you have been living as a paraplegic or quadriplegic ever since, you may have no sensation, spasm or movement at all. You no longer remember *how* to move, and your muscles are wasted. Even now, if you learn to think differently about your condition and are committed to improvement, you can achieve it. You will start by feeling slight sensations in the feet; later, in your ankles and calves; and with time and exercise to strengthen the muscles, the impulse to move or walk returns.

The effects of spinal cord injury vary from person to person even if the point of impact was the same. The limbs either become flaccid or tense. I believe the reason some injuries create spasticity and/or tension, and others create loose and flaccid limbs is connected to the moment of impact. It's also affected by your nature and the way you reacted when it happened.

Flaccid muscle

Wasting and shrinking occurs because you're not moving; muscle mass increases and tendons strengthen when you do. If your diet is such as to help you build muscle, and you focus your mind on moving, you will see improvement within three or four months.

Spasms

Spasms are alarming and (like any loss of control) can feel humiliating. As patients become more and more nervous about having them the slightest thing can set them off. Spasm medication is prescribed but as its effects wane, the spasm get worse.

Yet you can learn to relax and become free of the symptom. Spasms are purely a reaction to some barely noticeable stimulus. They are always unexpected, sporadic and out of your control – in other words they are not a physical effect of your injury but an unconscious drive towards movement – a drive that the central nervous system can't handle. The solution is to train your mind not to alert your body unnecessarily.

Why should your body go into spasm at certain moments? The likely explanation is that your mind is having a kind of flashback to the very second when your injury happened. Something about a sudden sound, a turn of the head or a particular look, takes you back to that moment. In a way spasms are a blessing as learning to control them is an important step towards your recovery.

Incontinence

Everyone with a spinal cord injury loses bladder and bowel control. The other bodily functions may remain and function intact and yet it seems that because you're told incontinence is inevitable and for life, tubes and catheters and bags are fitted and the bladder and bowel muscles get lazier. It doesn't take long before control is lost completely.

You can re-learn this. You have to think, but then you have to think about preparing to urinate or defecate anyway; as an able-bodied person, you naturally felt pressure and took control until it was convenient to release your waste products. I have found that people find this one of the easiest things to learn, probably because it's not involuntary or exhausting, yet they've always had to concentrate on what they were doing – it's not like walking.

An added advantage of re-learning bladder and bowel control is that you are exercising the muscles in your lower body and becoming aware of tension and flaccidity.

Depression

Becoming debilitated by injury makes you dependent on other people and this isn't what you want. At first, the restrictions are what you notice most. You will have to live your life in a new way and it's all unknown to you. Self-pity overwhelms you. This emotional shock, combined with the physical shock to your system, can so weaken you that for a while you lose hope.

These are facts, and tragically they can lead people to suicide. Others live in a state of depression to the end of their days. Depression can only reinforce paralysis and generate bitterness.

Then there are those who thrive. They accept their paralysis and life in a wheelchair, don't look back, and concentrate on developing all their mental and physical resources.

The point is: it's up to you. Whether or not you take control of your own mind is your own choice – you are the person who is going to have to put your decision into practice. The emotion you will use always exploit is hope. You will continue to aspire, never allow your hopes to be defeated and always remember that your mind and spirit remain unaffected by the injury and are *independent*. At first they may seem like the only parts of you that don't depend on others for help. Use them.

Instruct your mind to restore the power of your own will. Once you learn how to get in touch with your mind, you are doing things for yourself. Here's how to do it:

Refuse to accept any suggestion that you will never walk again.

Don't let anyone talk about this as a permanent disability.

Refuse to accept pity, commiseration or sympathy.

Practice breathing deeply and slowly *in* through your nose and *out* through your mouth. (When you first practise deep inward inhalation, thoughts will intrude. You will overcome this, as you increase the oxygen supply to your brain and learn to focus on your body.)

As you breathe in, imagine travelling with your breath, into your brain, down your spine, through your nerves, into the nerve endings until you reach the skin.

Now concentrate on your feet, and your toes. Breathe in and out *slowly* and in your imagination follow that breath to your brain and down to your feet.

Try to feel your limbs. Be aware of the slightest sensation.

In your imagination, magnify that sensation again and again.

Think about contracting the muscles in your feet.

Think about moving your toes, your ankles.

Do you feel a tingling sensation?

Your breathing exercises are beginning to prepare your mind to take control of your body.

Future developments

Stem cell research is just beginning. It offers hope to all spinal cord injury patients but decades may have to pass before these injuries can be 'cured' and full mobility restored to those who are now paralysed. At the moment stem cell treatment is a side-issue; a wonderful hope, but probably irrelevant to the majority. Even when, or if, stem cells do ultimately offer recovery, the emotional and mental effects of these injuries will still have to be dealt with and long and taxing exercise programmes undertaken to restore flagging muscles.

Sadly, I can predict from my own experience that if someone discovers a magic 'cure' for paralysis tomorrow, there will still be people who choose to remain in a wheelchair for life. The reason is simple. They find two hours of exercise a day too arduous and too difficult. They won't push themselves.

Stroke

A stroke takes place in one of two ways; either your brain is flooded with blood because blood pressure has become too high, or a blood clot prevents blood, with its oxygen supply, from getting to your brain at all. Either way, a stroke often results in loss of mobility or feeling, or both, on either the left or right side of the body. Tension can be so severe that it becomes impossible to open your fingers or your hand, or bend and flex your leg joints. Your muscles and tendons stiffen and you may lose the power of speech. Many functions are regained by therapy afterwards, but recovery is likely to be quicker and more enduring if the causes of mental tension are also addressed.

In general, stroke patients I've treated have been happy-go-lucky characters, although I have always noticed an element of suppressed anger. Having dealt with many cases, I have come to believe so much anger is being suppressed that the mind's only option is attack, experienced as an attack on the brain: a stroke.

It is futile to search your memory for a single event that may have triggered a stroke. You can't resolve past problems by re-living the pain they caused you. Simply live your life in the knowledge that anger (and its variants including resentment, retaliation, frustration and bitterness) should not be suppressed, because that way tension builds. You may not even recognise your anger, consciously, for what it is; sensitive people often bear with fortitude a constant, low level of psychological wounds and pinpricks. If you repeatedly suffer rejection, belittling and contempt, you get angry even if you don't show it, and the effect must eventually manifest itself somehow. No unresolved conflicts should be present in everyday life.

Maybe you have never learned to express your anger, or believe the consequences would be frightening and unbearable. But this depends how you handle it, and both negotiation and anger management skills can be learned. The first thing to do in a potentially combustible situation is calm yourself. Release past stresses and don't accept the pressure that other people's actions or words might place upon you. Particularly don't allow *your anger itself* to be belittled; it is what it is, a normal emotion, and you have no reason to be ashamed of it.

If you plunge blindly on with life while your emotions are in turmoil, progress becomes a constant battle. Organise your thoughts; decide what you want to achieve, the changes that will meet with resistance and how to overcome that resistance.

First learn to calm yourself at will. Breathing in through the mouth deeply and slowly will relax tense muscles. Ask yourself what tension you are feeling and why. What is worrying you? What makes you angry or afraid?

After a stroke you may be more tired than usual. This is not because you have been physically active but because your tensions are being released in sleep. Ask any healthy adult to hold just one side of their body in tension for five minutes – to make a tight left fist, twist the left side of their mouth, hold the foot rigid. They'll tell you that after five minutes they're exhausted. You, as a stroke victim, are doing that *all day*. Learning to relax your muscles is extremely important.

Recovery may seem slow. Avoid frustration. If you feel even the slightest irritation with yourself or anyone else, breathe deeply and you will detach from your anger. The more you practise, the more automatic this reaction will get.

What you are trying to do is remain calm at all times whether awake or asleep. You may expect other people to express sympathy. They mean well, but the obvious implication is that you're worse off than they are. This kind of thing can delay your rehabilitation, so avoid self-pity. Continue to exercise with determination, no matter how difficult it seems. Your brain has suffered damage but this can largely be made good, and whatever disability you are suffering doesn't have to be permanent.

Attitude

Learn to concentrate on the affected part of your body and will it to move. Even if one side of you is presently immobile, you must carry out this basic, focussing mental exercise if you are to trigger movement eventually.

Accept massage treatment for the taut, immobile side of your body as well as the side that is not affected.

Learn to push yourself. Recognise that tiring yourself out through exercise or manipulation is extremely beneficial as it leaves your muscles supple and relaxed.

Once you get moving, numbness goes and sensation increases. You feel more sensitive to touch and changes in temperature.

Traumatic brain injury

Several conditions already dealt with in this section result in traumatic brain injury. The cause may be injury from a blow, a fall or an accident; it may be Parkinson's or a stroke. In every case behaviour is affected. Most limitations can be repaired, in that your brain can be trained to make substitute connections.

The brain is driven by the mind and still responds to the patient's consciousness. It is the mind that we must pay attention to, for people can develop an ability to take instruction even if they are in a vegetative state. The more demands are placed upon them, the greater the chance of a response.

Manipulation

Deep breathing, to increase oxygen to the emotional centres of the brain, is fundamental. A person in a vegetative state can be helped to do it by manipulating their arms or legs. Explain what you're doing and give instructions; if you are pushing a limb ask them to push with you, and if you are pulling ask them to pull too. These instructions are extremely important because they trigger effort. Once you can generate effort, which will take persistence, you have the beginning of recovery. Exercises must be regular and at first, the more hours you can devote to the patient, the better.

The resulting tiredness makes them breathe more deeply and their brain is better able to receive instruction. The person may sigh or yawn instead of making an obvious effort to draw in breath; it doesn't matter. The important aspect is to increase air intake into the brain and body.

Head massage also helps. Whatever you try, your approach must be friendly with no suspicion of threat or intimidation. Instructions must be given in a firm, calm, clear but gentle voice. You are teaching reactions and behaviour as you would teach a child, in a strong, loving, compassionate and simple way.

Deep breathing offers liberation; the patient's hope and will to recover become visible. The capacity to move becomes, with practice, more active and more complex. I believe that if one can create even a small but definite improvement, this indicates the potential that is there. After that, continuing therapy is everything. Unfortunately it is impossible to predict a *rate* of progress; there may be a plateau which seems endless but is suddenly followed by a step to a higher level of achievement. As the carer, you must be prepared never to give up; always maintain a couple of hours of the exercise and breathing treatment daily.

In extreme brain injury cases it may be easy to assume that the person is in a vegetative state and cannot grasp sensory input of any kind, although with constant repetition you can obtain a response.

It is very hard for a parent or a partner to carry out this therapy. It may be possible, but you will need all your compassion, iron discipline and visible strength of will; only this strength in you can encourage your patient back to life. Weakness is catching, so if you are unready to stay the course, don't start.

Communication

Speech can be wholly or partly regained with exercise of the face and voice exercises. These also assist breathing and confidence.

However there may be many stages before speech. As soon there are some signs that the person is aware, tell her to lift her thumb for Yes and point her index finger for No, or get him to give two blinks for a Yes and one for No. Check for understanding and physical ability to reply ('Are these flowers red? Is this blanket blue?') and allow plenty of time for the response. *Be patient.* Their brain has to try a lot harder than yours does to make a response happen.

Talk normally. There is a tendency to treat everyone who's sick as though they're a hearing-impaired two-year-old. Never, ever, display irritation; the patient will shut down right away. All communications should be friendly and to the point – and this goes for everything you say around them, whether or not you are sure they can hear.

As for your own attitude to what you're doing: do it because you want to. It mustn't be a burden. Kind and loving, light hearted but strong is the idea.

Seizures

Often people with traumatic brain injury suffer seizures; when people are in no position to express themselves in the first place, the build-up of frustration must find some outlet. It is as if mind, brain and body collectively refuse to accept the burdens of the emotions.

Plenty of practice in breathing exercises will ease the onset of seizures and help with recovery. If you are present, don't show you are afraid and don't show you are uncertain. Sympathy is useless: breathing instructions can help in directing the mind back to the present. With time, it is possible to reduce the effect of the seizures and the recovery time.

Anti-convulsive drugs should be avoided, as these disable the brain's natural functions.

20 Yours and yours alone

Mastery of your mind

Be glad, for you have the greatest gift life has to offer. Your mind and brain are vastly more powerful than the world's most powerful supercomputer. Together they will help you do anything you want to do, and together they will seize every possible opportunity to improve and sustain you, body and soul.

Only when you learn to be inquisitive, to question your own mind and instruct it, do you fully comprehend the awesome possibilities within you. You can learn anything and do anything. You have an invisible faculty, unknown to anyone on earth and undiscoverable by anyone else: your mind. It is your mind that helps you to evolve and regenerate, to move on and adjust to circumstances. Treat it with respect. Let your consciousness ask your unconscious mind how to achieve all your goals in life. Conscious and unconscious are equal in unity.

Lose yourself in the darkness, filled with visions and patterns, that is projected into your unconscious; the answers you seek are there. Have no expectations. In due course, doors will open and obstacles will dwindle, leaving certainty and the freedom to achieve your goals. You will be transformed, refusing to be a victim no matter how weak or vulnerable you may have felt before. You will refuse to repeat mistakes, and this in itself will empower you, driving away all discomforts. You will refuse to submit, for by resistance your mind and body is empowered. You will refuse to torture yourself with the memory of pain inflicted by the words of others. Instead you will see their values for what they are, and be glad to know at first hand the consequences of unnatural behaviour.

You will see the sublime logic behind the actions produced by your well-instructed mind. You will see yourself objectively, dispassionately. You will value your own drive, and understand that all your qualities can be applied for good or ill depending on circumstances. Clear-sighted, unemotional, you will find yourself acting in your own interest to benefit others at the same time. This is the paradox of true balance.

Your mind is your eternal master.

Lightning Source UK Ltd.
Milton Keynes UK
UKOW04f0627250118
316812UK00001B/75/P

9 781911 110699